HUNTING AMERICA'S BEAR

Tactics for Taking Our Most
Exciting Big-Game Animal

AL RAYCHARD

The Lyons Press
Guilford, Connecticut
An imprint of The Globe Pequot Press

Dedicated to all the bear guides and outfitters I have hunted with over the years. I learned something from all of you.

The Lyons Press is an imprint of The Globe Pequot Press.

Printed in the United States of America

10 9 8 7 6 5 4 3 2 1

ISBN: 1-59228-397-7

Library of Congress Cataloging-in-Publication Data is available on file.

CONTENTS

ACKNOWLEDGMENTS v

INTRODUCTION 1

1. America's Bear 9

2. In the Bear Woods 31

3. Hunting Methods 71

4. Rifles and Cartridges 131

5. Bowhunting 153

6. Muzzleloaders and Slug Guns 169

7. Handgun Hunting 189

8. The Bear Seasons 197

9. Planning a Hunt 211

Appendix: Bear Hunting Resources 251

Selected Bibliography 273

Index 275

ACKNOWLEDGMENTS

It's a common misconception that authors of books such as this one are total experts on the subject discussed. While that is true in some cases, most of us are simply enthusiastic and passionate hunters who know what we know because of countless hours in the field over a period of years and because of the people we've been lucky enough to know along the way.

In a sense, this book was authored by dozens of people, including guides, outfitters, treehound enthusiasts, wildlife biologists, researchers, various organizations, and friends, to name but a few. All have contributed to my experiences with the black bear, and were kind enough to answer questions, offer opinions, provide information and data, and be there when this hunter needed them. I can be a pest at times, especially on deadline, and I thank you all for going above and beyond the call.

My love affair with the black bear is decades old now, and there are literally dozens of individual people and organizations, either directly or indirectly, that should be thanked here. Unfortunately, space does not allow it. I apologize for that, and I hope you know that you have my appreciation for what you taught me in some big or little way.

Special thanks, however, must go out to guide and outfitter Wayne Greene, who guided me to my first black bear those many years ago, to Joe Cabral of Russell Pond Outfitters, Don and Tuffy Ayers of Ayers Outfitting, Don and Rod Stowe of Mobile

Outfitters, Todd Wiseman of Newfoundland Adventures, Ron Parsons of Owl's Nest Lodge, and Denis Boivin of SEPAQ. Thanks also to Rock Agostino of Creative Maine Taxidermy, Jim Hackiewicz, and Jeff Folsom of *Bear Hunting Magazine.*

Thanks to biologists Jennifer Vashon, Maine Department of Inland Fisheries and Wildlife, and Craig McLaughlin, Utah Wildlife Resources. And to TRAFFIC North America, Washington D.C.; Center for Wildlife Information, Missoula, Montana; National Bowhunter Education Foundation, Townsend, Montana; U.S. Sportsmen's Alliance, Columbus, Ohio; and the Boone and Crockett Club, Missoula, Montana.

INTRODUCTION

I was sitting in a treestand some fifteen feet above the ground, high on a hardwood shelf on the western slope of Coburn Mountain in Somerset County, Maine, just a few miles south of the town of Jackman. It was early June 1976. Maine still had a spring bear season then, and I was on my first hunt for this species.

I really didn't know what to expect. My guide had told me the bait was being hit regularly, daily, in fact, and there was a good chance I'd see a bear. Despite the scent of the spring woods, the pleasant weather, and birds filling the air with song, the only thing I could think about was what he'd said. I had never seen a bear in the wild before—much less one just thirty yards away—yet here I was, alone, surrounded by wilderness, sitting over a bait intended to draw in an animal most folks hope never to see up close and personal, and the only thing between me and who knows what was a .54-caliber Lyman Great Plains Rifle loaded with 90 grains of blackpowder and a roundball. It didn't make much sense, and the longer I sat, the more I wondered what in the hell I'd gotten myself into.

Fortunately—at least that's what I thought at the time—I didn't have to wrestle with my emotions too long. About an hour after taking my position I leaned my head back against the tree in an attempt to relax and take in the smells and sounds. I closed my eyes, took some deep breaths, and released them ever so slowly. It seemed to work. Nothing had happened so far, and I began to think that if it did, everything would be all right. I continued to sit that way for several minutes, becoming increasingly more comfortable. I may even have snoozed for a few minutes, although in the back of my mind I could still hear the birds chirping away and chipmunks scurrying around on the ground near the bait. But then things changed.

Suddenly, there were no sounds. It was as if the volume on a radio had been turned down. No birds, no rustling on the forest floor. Nothing. Even the slight breeze that had been stirring the leaves seemed to die away. The change was so abrupt, so noticeable, that I immediately opened my eyes. And when I did, I was looking directly at a black bear standing broadside a few feet from the bait. My guide had been right. The animal had come down the ridge, silent as a ghost. It had given no indication of its presence. I didn't hear a thing.

Looking back now, I thank God I was a young man in good health, because my heart started to pound and my breath came in short spurts, as if I'd just finished the New York Marathon. The muzzleloader resting in my lap felt like an anvil. Then, as now, it's generally my nature to get excited when I see game, but not like this. This was a new sensation, completely different, more intense—and I liked it.

The bear stood motionless for several minutes, providing me an opportunity to study it closely. I was struck by how beautiful the black bear really is. When it proceeded toward the bait I found myself fascinated by its movement. It seemed to move with no effort, which surprised me in such a large animal. I sensed for the first time the great power of this animal, something that would continue to amaze me in the years to come. Once at the bait, it looked in my direction—right through me, or so I thought at the time—lifted its nose to test the wind, and then proceeded to eat. I found myself in total awe; the anxiety, questions, and doubts that had filled me earlier were completely gone. I was hooked, and have been ever since.

Since that first hunt many years ago, I have traveled from one end of North America to the other in pursuit of black bears, and even now, after countless spring and fall hunts, after observing literally hundreds of bears in different situations, it's difficult to put a finger on what so completely fascinates me. I can think of no single aspect that makes me enjoy studying and hunting this animal as much as I do. Rather, it's the whole picture, from the animal itself to where it lives. Whenever I'm in bear country, the juices flow and the excitement builds in a way that can't be compared to pursuing other game animals. I feel at home.

But I'm not alone in this high esteem. Since the beginning of time humankind has had a unique spiritual connection to the bear. Some of the earliest known religions were bear cults, and evidence of ritual burials have been noted in nearly every culture in the world. In many Native American cultures, the bear was so revered that it was forbidden to speak the word "bear." Instead, the animal was referred to by creative euphemisms. The Cree called the bear the "Angry One," "Big Hairy One," or "Good Tempered Beast," among other names. The Blackfoot also knew the bear as the "Good Tempered Beast," or the "Unmentionable One," while the Navaho referred to the bear as "He Who Lives in the Den," or "Reared in the Mountains." Many tribes referred to the bear in human terms, calling it cousin, brother, grandfather, or elder.

The skinned carcass of a black bear hanging from a game pole looks remarkably human, and it's not difficult to understand why Native Americans made the connection.

Perhaps the highest tribute to the human/bear relationship, however, are the myths and legends handed down through time in which the bear plays a pivotal roll. Many deal with how certain aspects of the natural world came to be, especially the constellations: Ursa Major and Ursa Minor (Latin for "Great Bear" and "Lesser Bear") and the Big Dipper and Little Dipper.

There is the Roman legend of Callisto, a young and beautiful nymph who had many suitors.

Thousands of years ago the gods were often known to appear as mortals. Jupiter (Zeus in Greek mythology) was king of the gods, and he was well known for being unfaithful to his wife, Juno (or Hera). So it came to pass that Jupiter took a liking to Callisto, appeared to her, and soon she bore a child, Arcas. The birth of the child made Juno realize that her husband had been unfaithful, and in her blind anger she brought down divine wrath upon Callisto, decreeing that the woman should live as a bear, forever cursed to wander the wilds like an animal.

Callisto's hands twisted into massive paws, and her body grew a coat of fur. She grew fat, and her face pressed into a shortened muzzle. The beautiful woman had become a great and terrible bear. Arcas was devastated at the disappearance of his mother, for he did not realize she had been cursed, and Juno made certain that he did not discover this.

For many years, Callisto wandered the forests and plains. She was terrified when night came, because she didn't know how to be a bear. She had been a young nymph all her life, and now the sounds and smells of the forest filled her with fear. Even other bears and the animals of the woods scared her. This was not the worst of her troubles, though. She was a magnificent bear, and many hunters sought to capture her and claim her hide.

Arcas grew up to be a powerful hunter, perhaps the greatest hunter in the world. He spent many hours each day in the wilderness hunting deer and other animals. It was only natural that he would decide to claim the prize of this great bear's hide. One day, he came upon the great bear while out hunting. She was drinking water from a stream and did not see him. Unaware that the animal was actually his mother, Arcas pulled out an arrow and waited for the best moment to fire.

Jupiter, who normally paid little or no attention to his old lovers, took pity on the pair. Seeing that Arcas was about to release his arrow, Jupiter changed him into a bear and hauled mother and son into the heavens by their tails. It is for this reason that both Ursa Major and Ursa Minor have long tails. They remain frozen in space, Arcas the bear still holding his bow in clumsy paws.

The punishment was not yet over, for Juno was still filled with anger. She sought out Oceanus and Tethys, the controllers of the sea, and made a request. She asked that the two bears never be allowed to sink below the sea to rest like the other inhabitants of the sky.

And then there is the Iroquois legend of The Three Bears.

Long ago, the Great Bear wandered freely throughout the sky. His massive paws took him far across the unlimited ceiling of the world. He hunted and fished, finding food in the many rivers of the sky. All throughout the first spring he did this, until his belly was full and he felt happy.

He did not know that three young braves had discovered him feeding that spring. They sought his pelt and meat to feed their families in the long winter they knew was coming soon. Without warning, the braves ran out after the bear, trying to catch and kill him. The Great Bear ran to escape the hunters. All through the long summer he ran, always trying to get away. The braves, however, were very cunning and strong. Eventually, they caught up with him. In the first autumn, their arrows pierced the Great Bear and he died. The blood of the bear spilled out of the sky and tinged all the leaves with red and orange. The trees then dropped their leaves in mourning for their friend, the Great Bear.

The Great Bear was reborn the following spring, as is the way with bears, and the braves set out after him again. They do this each year. If you watch the sky, you can see the three braves trailing behind the Great Bear as he runs toward the horizon.

On many a night in spring bear camp I have looked toward the heavens and found the Great Bear of which these myths speak. It's not difficult. The bowl stars of the Big Dipper form the bear in Native American legends, while the stars represent the hunters chasing it. Alternatively, the "handle" is the tail of the bear, the bowl part of the hindquarters. On a clear night, if you locate the two stars forming the beginning of the bowl and follow along the line they make you can find the North Star, Polaris. The star forms part of the tail of the Lesser Bear, and was used by sailors as a guide to finding their direction at night. The phrase "getting your bearings" comes from the practice of using the Great Bear to find the North Star.

Whether you believe in such things, or even wonder about them, as I have and often do, there is little doubt the bear remains a topic of interest among hunters. If this weren't the case, the bear would not be the second most hunted big game animal on the continent, drawing an estimated 300,000 to 400,000 hunters into the field each year. These hunters take about 40,000 bears, which means that only the whitetail surpasses the bear in total annual harvest. Not everyone thinks about this animal with reverence or awe, but I'm willing to bet the house that the mere sight or presence of a bear would stir emotions seldom felt. After hunting them for more than a quarter century, I still get just as excited as I did on that first hunt.

Much of this exhilaration stems from the fact that it's difficult to predict what will happen while hunting black bears. Over time, the bear's reputation has largely been built on rumor and innuendo that paints it as everything from a man killer to a gentle giant. In my experience, the truth lies somewhere in the middle. After encountering scores of bears while hunting—up close in a good many cases—I have never felt threatened or been in fear for my life. I do, however, give the bear a great deal of respect, and try never to underestimate it.

There have been a couple of occasions, largely my own fault, when I've had to give a bear room. The potential for dangerous encounters is enough to get folks thinking. This fact, along with the bear's potential size and beauty, make it such an interesting and exciting quarry for the modern hunter. And in many areas, it's the only major game animal that can be hunted during a spring season.

As you read these words, there's a good chance I'll be in a bear camp somewhere, perhaps sitting in a stand, following a pack of hounds, or glassing a distant hillside. Even if I'm stuck at home, the black bear will not be long out of my thoughts. This is a unique, special animal, and still a mystery to me in more ways than one. That is why I'm so enchanted with them, why I still get excited just being where they are, and why I'll never be able to stay away.

Chapter

1

AMERICA'S BEAR

It's early September in northern Idaho's Bitterroot Mountains, and with binoculars in hand I'm sitting against an ancient slab of granite overlooking a burn across a ravine. A stream cascades somewhere down below; other than a slight breeze passing through the nearby trees, it's the only sound I hear.

Like much of the West, these mountains have witnessed forest fires more than once over the years, but what fire takes away it gives back in abundance. The area across the way no doubt looked devastated at some point in the recent past, but now an extensive patchwork of huckleberry (a seedless, juicy fruit much like a blueberry) covers the landscape. The fruit is a favorite food of man and wildlife alike, especially black bears. There seems to be a bumper crop this fall, which is why I've ventured a mile above camp on this particular morning hoping to spot a bear.

After an hour of glassing and wondering if I should move on, my patience is finally rewarded. Out of the woods to the east emerge a sow and two cubs no larger than bushel baskets, obviously born that winter. The cubs run about, investigating this and that, curious and unsuspecting in their youth, and then begin to feast on the smorgasbord of wild berries. But the mother just stands there.

Through my 10x50 binoculars, I make note of how she occasionally lifts her nose to test the wind, looks left then right, and then slowly lumbers forward to join her cubs. It's a spectacular and exciting scene, and as I settle in to watch as long as possible, I wish I had a cup of coffee to help complete the best show in town.

That sow didn't know it, of course, but she is part of a long lineage dating back more than 500,000 years on this continent. Following the same route across the Bering Land Bridge as the tremarctine, or short-faced, bears twelve million years earlier, the ancestors of the black bear entered present-day Alaska, and over the next millennia slowly spread out across North America. Eventually, what we now generally classify as *Ursus americanus*, the black bear, made this continent its exclusive home. It's found nowhere else on earth—truly an "American Bear."

From the beginning, life for the new bear was not easy. As a defensive measure, it learned to climb trees, the only North American bear that readily does so. And since it couldn't compete for food with larger bears or drive competitors away from its kills, the black bear did what it does best. It adapted. The new world was blessed with a wealth of other foods such as fruits, nuts, insects, bees and honey, various succulents and other plants, carrion and small rodents, even fish, and the black bear took advantage of it all, becoming an opportunistic omnivore in the process.

It's a trait for which the black bear is well known today. Early French *voyageurs* called the bear *Cochons de bois*, or "Pigs of the Woods," and the term seems fitting. Black bears will eat just about anything, but they are generally selective feeders much of the time, "seeking out the most digestible and highly nutritional foods in season," according to authors Jeff Fair and Lynn Rogers in *The Great American Bear.*

Black bears have adapted well to their environment, becoming omnivores that will eat virtually anything.

I knew this to be true. I was actually booked in Idaho on a bait hunt, and while an offering of sweets and meats does a good job of drawing in bears, I had been told by outfitter Joe Cabral of Russell Pond Outfitters that there was a good crop of berries on this fall, and the bears were only hitting the bait sporadically. This proved to be the case during the first few days of my trip, which is why I had ventured to the ridge above camp that morning. More than once over the years bears had shown me their preference for natural foods over handouts, so I wasn't surprised to spot the sow and cubs.

This willingness to take advantage of a wide variety of foods, along with its adaptability, has allowed the black bear to expand its range, and to actually thrive while other bears succumbed to changing times. During the past few ice ages bears and many other species were forced south into small habitats by expanding ice sheets. Many species disappeared, including the tremarctine bears, and until the arrival of the grizzly bear, the black bear was probably the only species of bear in North America.

It was around this time, about two million years ago, that the black bear is believed to have separated into two lineages, with populations moving into the continent's fragmented eastern and western forests. Later, about 350,000 years ago, the western group separated into a coastal group and interior group, which subsequently diverged into four coastal subspecies: *Ursus americanus kermodei, U. a. carlotte, U. a. vancouveri,* and *U. a. altifrontalis.*

Today, these subspecies are still with us. The subspecies *carlotte* is found on the Queen Charlotte Islands, the subspecies *vancouveri* on Vancouver Island, and the subspecies *kermodei,* or spirit bear, primarily on Princess Royal Island, all off the coast of British Columbia. The subspecies *altifrontalis* ranges the Pacific Northwest.

Eastern bear populations were also segregating. Two subspecies still present are the Florida black bear, *Ursus americanus floridanus* and the Louisiana black bear, *Ursus americanus lutedus.* At one time, the Florida subspecies ranged throughout much of the Florida panhandle north to the coastal plains of southern Georgia and Alabama, numbering perhaps 12,000 animals. Due to loss of habitat, however, its population has dropped to about 1,500, and it has been listed as threatened by the state of Florida since 1974. Due to continuous development and habitat degradation, its future is bleak. Today, it's primarily found on national forest lands and surrounding public and private lands.

The Louisiana subspecies once roamed throughout much of that state, neighboring Mississippi, and into east Texas. It now numbers probably less than one hundred animals, although that figure is improving, and efforts are underway to restore the subspecies and expand its range. Since 1992 the Louisiana black bear has been listed as threatened by the U.S. Fish and Wildlife Service under the Endangered Species Act. The designation also covers bears in Mississippi and east Texas due to their similarities.

Today, taxonomists generally separate black bears into sixteen subspecies based on minor differences in appearance and DNA. Along with the ones mentioned above, these include *U. a. amblyceps* in the Southwest; *U. a. americanus*, found from Alaska to the Atlantic Ocean; *U. a. californiensis*, found in interior California; *U. a. cinnamomum*, found in parts of British Columbia, Alberta, and Manitoba and parts of Wyoming, Colorado, Idaho, and western Montana; *U. a. emmonsii*, found in coastal Alaska from Glacier Bay to Prince Edward Sound; *U. a. eremicus*, in northeastern Mexico and the Big Bend area of Texas; *U. a. hamiltoni* of Newfoundland; *U. a. machetes* in northwestern Mexico, *U. a. perniger* on the Kenai Peninsula of Alaska; and *U. a. pugnax* of southeastern Alaska.

The Louisiana subspecies is listed as threatened, but elsewhere in North America populations remain strong. (USFWS)

In years to come, this list will undoubtedly grow as taxonomists continue to update subspecies classifications based on regional differences in DNA, form, and behavior.

One of the more interesting aspects among these various subspecies is the difference in markings and color. The white blaze on the chest of some black bears is not a universal characteristic, and is insignificant or missing entirely in some populations, particularly in the West. The brown shading along the sides and bridge of the nose is generally longer and lighter, or at least less pronounced, on eastern bears.

And then there are the so-called color-phase, off-color, or colored black bears—whichever you decide to call them. The

Many black bears have white markings on the chest, but it's not a universal characteristic.

kermodei black bear of coastal British Columbia and some off-shore islands, first described for science by Dr. William Hornady of the New York Zoo in 1905, is nearly white, although not an albino. Instead of the pink eyes of an albino, its eyes are actually brown. The "glacier bear" found near Glacier Bay in southeast Alaska and parts of nearby Canada is blue or bluish-gray.

While both colorations appear only infrequently in populations that are predominately black, in parts of the West, particularly in an arc from northern California to Manitoba and down the backbone of the Rocky Mountains into New Mexico and Arizona, various color phases of black bears include brown (chocolate), blonde, and cinnamon.

The percentage of colored bears in each area varies, but in some locales it appears quite high, perhaps as much as 40 to 60 percent. Studies into this phenomenon are few and far between at the state or province level, but one recent study in southeast Colorado put the number of brown-phase black bears at 80 percent. Perhaps the best indicator of the availability of colored bears in a given area comes from hunters. Outfitter Don Ayers, who operates a string of remote tent camps east of Fort McMurray in northeast Alberta, once told me that 20 to 30 percent of the bears taken by his clients annually are some color other than black. Joe Cabral, an outfitter operating in the St. Joe and Clearwater National Forests of northern Idaho, reports his bear kills at nearly 50 percent off-color.

These figures are based on actual bear harvests, so I take them as fairly accurate. Whatever the case, it's certainly not uncommon for guides and outfitters in much of the West to post respectable numbers of colored black bears each year.

Except in parts of the upper Midwest like Minnesota, where bear researcher Lynn Rogers states he saw brown fur on one of every twenty to thirty bears during his extensive studies, and on rare occasion in the East, such as two bears tagged at a station in Pennsylvania in the late 1970s and a dark brown specimen taken in the Blue Hill area of Maine a few years ago, color phasing seem to be largely a Western phenomenon. This is where hunters seeking such bears should concentrate their efforts, based on contacts with area guides, outfitters, and state/provincial wildlife biologists.

From a biological perspective, color phasing is rather interesting. While the research is ongoing, one common consensus is that it evolved as a protective measure during times when western black bears shared home ground with grizzly bears and other now-extinct bear populations that were brown. Another is that the

Color-phase bears are common in many areas of the West.

coloring serves to keep bears cool while feeding on the exposed "balds" and living in the more open terrain of the West. As the bear is covered with a heavy coat of fur and is known to be fond of taking a dip in cool water during the heat of summer (black absorbs more solar heat), the theory makes sense.

Whatever the true cause, phasing may change on an individual at some point in its life. While sitting on a bait in Idaho recently, I observed a small female that was actually part black and part brown. I don't know if she was in the process of changing color or not, but it was a most unusual sight. Coloring is also genetically inherited, and parents that are colored, or were colored at some point in their life, are more apt to produce colored offspring. Litters may even be mixed, with some brown, or other shade, and some black.

A color-phase black bear is considered a true trophy by many hunters. Some pursue such bears with a special passion; not necessarily due to their rarity, but simply because they are unusual.

The black bear is the smallest of all North American bears. The adult male, called a boar, can weigh 130 to over 600 pounds. Although bigger examples have been recorded, including a monstrous 802-pounder taken in Wisconsin in 1885, males larger than 500 pounds are not overly common, despite what is often written and advertised. Even in wilderness areas and regions with light hunting pressure, any boar from around 375 to 450 pounds that measures between six and seven feet from nose to tail, and any female in the 250- to 300-pound class, is a real prize.

The heaviest recorded wild male tipped the scales at 902 pounds, the heaviest female 520 pounds, and both were checked at peak fall weight. In height, measured from the bottom of the pads while flat on the ground to the highest point on the shoulder, males generally run up to three feet, perhaps a bit more.

On average, females, or sows, run 20 to 60 percent smaller than males. Sows are typically shorter in height, and most weigh under 200 pounds, perhaps slightly more in prime condition when living in good habitat. Despite their size and lumbering gait—and the body hair and fur that tends to make them overheat and tire quickly—both sexes can sprint at speeds up to thirty miles per hour, climb trees with great ease, and run uphill or down with the same ease as on level ground.

The largest black bears are most often taken in remote areas of the far north and west, where hunting pressure is minimal and bears can reach a ripe old age, but they also show up in areas to the east, especially from Pennsylvania south along the middle and southern Appalachians, where living conditions are better. In eastern areas, the availability of natural foods like beechnut and acorns and the mixture of agricultural foods contribute greatly to the bear's better-than-average size.

The black bear is the smallest North American bear. Large males weigh up to 600 pounds, while a large female might tip the scales at 300 pounds.

The hibernation period is also shorter in the Southeast, which means bears are active and feeding for a longer period of time each year. Pennsylvania is considered to have some of the best bear habitat on the continent, with bears in the 300- to 400-pound range common. Parts of Virginia, and especially the Carolinas, also produce some of the largest black bears anywhere. On average, both sexes are larger in the East than the West for this reason, although large specimens are found throughout their range.

During hibernation, both sexes can lose 20 to 30 percent of their body weight, which is why bears harvested in the fall are always heavier than those taken in the spring. Hunters should also keep in mind that field dressing removes 10 to 20 percent of body weight; the bigger the bear, the smaller the percentage.

In outward appearance, older sows of young-rearing age look somewhat leaner and not as bulky, or muscular, as boars. While they're generally not as big or heavy, their hindquarters often look a bit wider, undoubtedly from giving birth. The face is also generally longer and narrower, more dog-like. These are slight differences, however, and discerning males from females in the wild is always difficult. This is partly true because both sexes always appear larger than they are, which leads hunters to exaggerate the size of their harvest. Throughout much of their range, particularly in areas with heavy hunting pressure, the average bear taken by hunters these days seems to run between 150 and 250 pounds.

All bears are covered with a blanket of thick hair, called guard hair. These hairs are usually three or four inches long, and their primary purpose is to provide camouflage and protection from moisture and insect bites and stings, which is why bears can steal honey from beehives and reside in blackfly- and mosquito-infested habitat with near impunity.

Beneath this outer guard hair, next to the skin, is a thick layer of guard fur that provides warmth. During its prime in late

This large boar weighed 468 pounds, but bears of this size aren't common.

fall through the early weeks of spring, guard fur is almost wool-like and measures 1¼ to 1½ inches long. This underfur is shed annually, generally starting in mid to late spring. When bears rub, they are probably trying to remove this fur, along with scratching the itch from dry skin just below.

For this reason, the best time to harvest a bear in its prime in most northern areas is April, May, the first two weeks of June, and again after late September. These layers of guard hair and under-fur make bears look bigger and give prime pelts a fuller, thicker appearance.

Under all this fur is a rather small, almost human-like body. It is still heavily muscled and big-boned, and in the late fall, just before entering the den, can carry a generous layer of fat several inches thick, but relative to its overall appearance there isn't a lot of body under there. Hunters should always keep this in mind, as it makes shot placement critical.

Females reach sexual maturity at three or four years of age, and males a year or so later. Mating can occur any time from June through early August depending on the locale, and the pair may remain together for several hours or several days. Before and after mating season, the black bear is a solitary creature, except for sows with cubs.

Once mating is complete, the fertilized egg remains dormant and does not implant in the uterus until the fall. Cubs are born blind, with blue eyes that will eventually turn brown. They're also toothless, nearly hairless, and weigh about half a pound.

Cubs usually arrive sometime in January or early February after a gestation of about seven months, while still in the den. Males and females in the litter are usually split 50/50, with the total number varying from one to five, although larger litters have been recorded. Two cubs seem to be the average across much of the West, with three the Eastern norm. The most I have ever observed is four (in Maine).

By April or May, after a continuous diet of mother's milk that is much higher in solids, total fats, and proteins than cow's milk, the cubs weigh about five pounds and are ready to leave the den. By fall they may run 15 to 80 pounds, depending on the availability and quality of food. Although weaning takes place at six to eight months, cubs typically remain with their mothers for about a year and a half, sometimes longer, again depending on the food supply. When food is scarce, the female can abort its blastocysts, embryos, or fetuses, and mating may be delayed for three or four years.

Black bears can live for twenty or thirty years in the wild, but few make it that far, except in remote locations. Young cubs

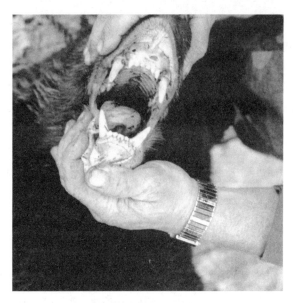

A black bear has forty-two teeth, including large upper and lower canines that allow it to utilize many types of food. Aging is normally conducted using the smaller premolars behind the canines.

under seventeen months often fall victim to predation, starvation or accident, and in many areas are killed by hunters. Across North America, the average age of a black bear at death in hunted areas is three to five years.

Assuming they survive, the sow forces her young to stop traveling with her about a week before mating. From that point on they are pretty much on their own. Most will remain within their mother's home area throughout their lives, typically an area covering anywhere from two to two hundred square miles. By this time the youngsters will have learned everything they need to survive in the wilds, primarily what to eat and where to find it, what is dangerous and how to seek safety.

Though normally quiet, they'll even possess a vocal repertoire, including bawls, grunts, growls, moans, chops, huffs, clacking of teeth, and blows, all used to express a range of emotions from pleasure to fear. Contrary to what we see in the movies and read in magazines, the black bear has a shy, elusive demeanor. Even sows accompanied by cubs rarely threaten by growling. In most cases, particularly when humans are involved, bears are more inclined to escape than attack, often fleeing an area long before they can be seen.

Both sexes of adult have a tail, although it's short at about two inches, and in many cases it's barely noticeable.

One of the biggest misconceptions about black bears, particularly sows, is that they attack humans in defense of cubs. Although any black bear should be dealt with cautiously, attacks on humans are rare. Use good sense, and give the bear ground whenever possible, particularly around food sources. Attacks do happen, but aggressively defending cubs is more of a grizzly trait. Black bears may take up a threatening posture, particularly in defense of food, but unless provoked or spooked they rarely follow through.

The black bear has a large brain compared to body size and is considered one of the more intelligent mammals. Its navigational skills are far superior to those in humans, and they possess excellent long-term memory. Once a reliable food supply is discovered, they are unlikely to forget it and will often travel many miles to reach it. They have fair-to-good vision under a hundred yards or so, can detect movement extremely well, and see color, so camouflaged clothing and sitting still or moving cautiously helps when hunting them. Officially, their long-range vision is untested, but I have spooked bears at distances greater than two hundred yards on spot-and-stalk hunts. Of course, I can never be certain whether my scent, noise, movement, or a combination of these things actually gave me away.

It is known, however, that black bears have extremely keen hearing and smelling capabilities. Both are considered among

Bears use their extraordinary sense of smell to locate food and assess danger.

their most important defenses. Their hearing exceeds human frequency and most likely has twice the sensitivity. Their nasal mucosa area (the area in the nose that allows all creatures to detect smell and at what level) is about a hundred times larger than in humans, and a black bear's sense of smell is estimated to be seven times greater than a bloodhound's.

They also have an organ on the roof of their mouths called a Jacobson's organ, which further enhances the sense of smell. Black bears have been observed traveling for a mile or more in a straight line to locate a food source, and monitored at up to thirty miles for the same purpose. They love water, swim well, and often take a dip to cool off during the heat of summer, sometimes swimming over a mile in fresh water.

One of the more interesting aspects of the black bear is its period of hibernation. Starting in mid-August in most areas—sooner in the north where reliable food sources are less abundant and the seasons short—the black bear enters a period called hyperphagia, which in layman's terms means they commence a feeding frenzy. In order to lay on the fat that will carry them through winter, the bear changes its diet from leaves and insects to fruits, nuts, and other foods high in fat and carbohydrates.

Unless these foods are present in the immediate area, it's not unusual for a bear to migrate twenty to fifty miles between summer and fall feeding range. These areas are generally low-elevation habitats or areas recovering from a burn or logging operations, where brambles and other berry-producing plants are among the first to appear. In spring and summer, bears typically forage for two to four hours in early morning and late afternoon into the night. But during hyperphagia, active feeding may go on for twenty hours a day, even during broad daylight, and it's not unusual for a bear to gain as much as thirty pounds a week.

When a bear actually enters its den varies from area to area, but contrary to common belief the process isn't triggered by cold weather or shortening daylight hours, but rather by lack of food. In fact, the length and duration of hibernation is genetically programmed to match food supplies. For that reason, hibernation is deeper and longer in northern areas where reliable food is available only from May through August or September; it can last up to seven or eight months in some regions.

In southern areas, where food is often available year-round, bears may not hibernate at all, and if they do, they may leave their dens for short periods or are easily aroused. Females typically hibernate longer than males because they're suckling cubs, retiring earlier in the fall and emerging later in the spring.

Gradually but steadily throughout the fall, as food quantity and quality dwindles, bear activity levels drop until food supplies are gone. By then, activity ceases completely, metabolism rates drop, and bears head for their dens, which often consist of nothing more than a burrow, cave, hollowed-out log, or rock crevice just large enough to shelter them.

Once in the den, a black bear will not eat, drink, or defecate for the duration. Although the kidneys continue to function, the small amount of water is reabsorbed into the body and there is a slight buildup of uric acid in the blood. Through the winter, a bear loses heat slowly, generally maintaining body temperatures at around 88 degrees Fahrenheit, which is within twelve degrees of their summer body temperature. This enables them to cut metabolic rates dramatically. Heart beats range from forty or fifty per minute for a short time after first entering the den to eight beats per minute when in deep sleep. Sows may rouse from their slumber to tend newborn cubs, but they generally resume hibernation quickly.

Because of the black bear's slow reproduction rate, the North American population as a whole has never possessed the ability to increase rapidly, although it has enjoyed large numbers. There were probably around two million black bears in the 1500s. Since the arrival of European settlers, however, the black bear/human relationship has always been tenuous at best. Until modern studies shed light on its true nature, the bear was the victim of a poor, and largely unjust, reputation.

In times past it has been hunted and trapped without protection of game laws, even bountied in many states to control numbers or eradicate it completely. As a result, and as bear habitat was gobbled up for human uses, the black bear had disappeared or been greatly reduced in number by the early 1900s throughout much of its native range.

Today, we have a much better understanding of the black bear. In all states and provinces where it can be legally hunted, it enjoys protective status under game or wildlife laws. Now it is ex-

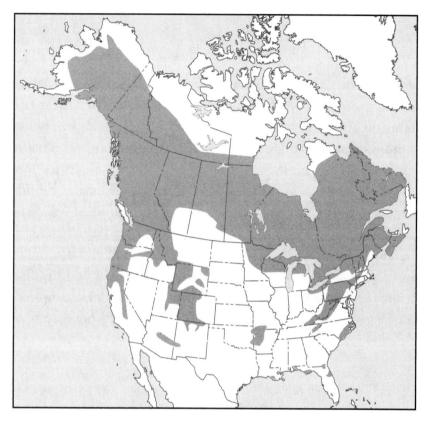

Black bear distribution.

panding its range, and populations are stable or increasing just about everywhere in its present range. Resident black bear populations are known to exist in at least forty-one of the fifty U.S. states and eleven of the twelve Canadian provinces and territories. Despite dwindling habitat in some states, black bear numbers are on the rise, and even in states that list bear populations as unknown, there is increasing evidence of small remnant populations and some cross-border migration. Black bears may actually be present in as many as forty-five states.

Since its arrival, the black bear has always been the most common and widely distributed bear on the North American continent, and so it remains today. Overall distribution includes most of Canada, with only one province (Prince Edward Island), having no bear population. In the United States black bears are found in Alaska, along the mountainous west coast, the Rocky Mountains southward to northern Mexico, in certain states of the upper Midwest, from New England southward along the Appalachians into northern Georgia, in fragmented areas of Florida westward through the Gulf States, Texas, and northeast Arkansas.

Historically, black bears rarely ranged above tree line, but in increasing numbers they are being reported on the tundra and in northern areas where forests don't exist. While caribou hunting in the Torngat Mountains of far northern Labrador a couple of years ago, just a few miles in from the sea and well above tree line

While a black bear's claws are well adapted for climbing trees, the species is sometimes found in treeless areas.

I watched a large black bear dine on blueberries for over an hour. I have also observed them above tree line in other areas east and west of Hudson Bay.

According to TRAFFIC, an international wildlife trade monitoring network, as of 1996, the most recent continent-wide figures available, the total North American population was estimated at 339,000 to 465,000 black bears in the United States and 396,000 to 476,000 in Canada, for a total of between 735,000 and 941,000 animals. Considering the fact that many states and provinces report their populations as stable to increasing, and few report decreasing populations, the actual estimate today is probably closer to one million.

ESTIMATED BLACK BEAR POPULATIONS

State or Province	Reported Population
Alabama	50
Alaska	100,000–200,000
Arizona	2,000–3,000
Arkansas	3,000
California	17,000–23,000
Colorado	10,000–12,000
Connecticut	30–60
Delaware	0
Florida	1,000–1,500
Georgia	1,800–2,000
Hawaii	0
Idaho	20,000–25,000
Illinois	0
Indiana	0
Iowa	0
Kansas	0
Kentucky	25–75
Louisiana	300
Maine	22,000–23,000
Maryland	250–300
Massachusetts	1,200–1,500
Michigan	12,000

State or Province	Reported Population
Minnesota	20,000
Mississippi	50
Missouri	100–200
Montana	20,000
Nebraska	0
Nevada	200–400
New Hampshire	2,500–3,000
New Jersey	550–700
New Mexico	4,000
New York	4,000–5,000
North Carolina	8,500
North Dakota	10
Ohio	12–30
Oklahoma	100–150
Oregon	25,000–30,000
Pennsylvania	7,500
Rhode Island	0–2
South Carolina	275
Tennessee	900–1,200
Texas	75–100
Utah	800–1,200
Vermont	2,500
Virginia	3,000–3,500
Washington	30,000
West Virginia	5,000–6,000
Wisconsin	14,000
Wyoming	Unknown
Alberta	40,000
British Columbia	120,000–160,000
Manitoba	25,000–30,000
New Brunswick	14,000
Newfoundland	6,000–10,000
Nova Scotia	8,000
Northwest Territories	10,000
Ontario	75,000–100,000
Prince Edward Island	0
Quebec	60,000
Saskatchewan	24,000
Yukon Territory	Unknown

Chapter

2

IN THE BEAR WOODS

I often get asked about my favorite aspect of bear hunting. And I'm sure my answer surprises a lot of hunters, because actually filling tags with trophy bears matters less to me than where bear hunting takes me. My soul belongs to the deep woods, the swamps and mountain ridges—the more remote and less trammeled the better. I feel at ease there, and there's no place I'd rather be. The black bear also loves this type of country, which I like to think makes us kindred spirits in that respect.

Having said that, though, I have to admit that my interest in the black bear is purely self-serving; I always have one objective in mind. I am a hunter, one who loves hunting bears in particular, and setting my sights or pulling full draw on a respectable black bear is what the game is all about.

As many of us discovered early on, or should have, any hunter ignorant of how, when, and why his quarry uses a given area is at a major disadvantage. The more you know about an animal, the better your chances of success. And with the black bear's keen sense of smell and hearing and its shy behavior, this becomes particularly important. With such assets at its disposal, it's not surprising that we seldom see bears, even though they often reside remarkably close to major human population centers. Knowing their likes and needs will lead hunters to more sightings, which translates into more opportunities.

Sitting over bait or trailing a pack of hounds greatly increases the chances of spotting and killing a bear, but in many areas those practices are illegal, making spot-and-stalk the only viable hunting method. In order to do it successfully, we must learn to identify the signs bears leave behind—tracks, scat or droppings, and markings on trees—what draws them to certain locales, what keeps them there, and what they prefer to eat.

Even where baiting and the use of dogs are legal, knowing where a bear is apt to concentrate its feeding forays at a particular time of year, and where it is traveling, can dictate where to establish baits or where to commence tracking with hounds. Time spent observing and learning the key factors that influence the bear's daily routine throughout spring, summer, and fall will pay dividends when you head afield with gun or bow in hand.

FOOD

The black bear is a professional and full-time feeder. Except during its winter sleep and a few weeks during the mating season around late June, the black bear spends every waking hour attempting to satisfy its perpetual hunger. From a hunting perspective, if you locate favorite foods, you'll find more bears.

During the winter months, a bear's metabolism drops only slightly below normal summer rates, the end result being that it merely goes into a deep sleep while hibernating. Nearly as much food energy is utilized each day in the den as when active the rest of the year, which is why a bear loses so much weight during the winter. This means that when a black bear emerges from the den in spring it is immensely hungry and immediately begins to eat, although gradually at first and generally on grasses to help recondition the stomach and intestines to food.

The problem is that spring and summer foods found naturally in the wilds are not as abundant as they will be in late summer and fall, and aren't as nutritious. Even in areas where bears live near orchards and agricultural lands, such foods are not yet available. And because they are so active in feeding once they emerge from the den, covering a lot of ground and using energy in the process, they continue to lose weight throughout the spring and much of the summer. It is only in late summer and fall that they experience a serious weight gain, largely because of a greater abundance of highly nutritious foods.

Hunters, whether afield in spring or fall, must understand that food sources are seasonal by nature, and that their relative abundance varies depending on habitat, geography, and weather conditions. Knowing what these foods are, when they become available, and where they can be found will lead you to more bears.

Black bears will move from area to area based on the availability of food, traveling great distances to find it. The home range of this animal can extend up to two hundred square miles, and while bears prefer to remain within their established turf, when food is scarce it's not uncommon for either sex, even sows with cubs, to travel outside of their range to forage. Even if they remain within their home area, it's not unusual for a bear to ramble fifteen to twenty miles a day to locate a reliable food supply.

Males typically have a larger core range than females, perhaps sixty to ninety square miles compared to roughly fifteen to thirty square miles, and therefore will travel greater distances as conditions warrant. This makes exploring and scouting bear country a time-consuming endeavor, as many miles must be covered in the process.

This large boar was taken during the spring season and weighed in at 300 pounds. In the fall, it might have been much heavier.

Black bears don't act like deer and other hoofed big game we have come to know well. Once a bear depletes a food source, it simply moves on. And as the gastrointestinal tract of a bear is much larger than that of other true carnivores—a two-hundred-pound bear can consume several pounds or more of berries or meat at one sitting—depleting a food source generally doesn't take long. The bear also excretes waste rather quickly, another reason they eat much of the time.

Deer might stay close to a particular acorn or beechnut ridge for several weeks, perhaps a month, but a bear might be in such an area for only a week or less. They may move just a mile to another productive ridge or ten miles to feed on blueberries, but once the immediate source is gone, so are they.

Hunters should always be on the lookout for food sources, because more times than not that is where bears will be. Remember, too, that black bears like to be near water. Under normal weather conditions throughout their range, black bears must drink at least twice each day, even more during dry spells, so a bear's core area will always have several reliable watering holes—a river, stream, lake, pond, or sometimes nothing more than a spring.

While the black bear is considered omnivorous, meaning it will take advantage of just about any food matter, it's basically a meat-eater that learned to augment its diet with a wide variety of plants, fruits, and nuts. Unlike hoofed mammals, the black bear's digestive system is not well suited to breaking down cellulose, so it must seek out the highest quality plants that are easy to digest and offer the most nutritional value.

Black bears consume a wide variety of foods, including grains, corn, and other domestic food crops.

In the mountainous West, plants like the glacier lily, sedges, horsetails, and members of the pea family, to name but a few, often emerge first and grow much faster on south-facing slopes in higher elevations. The younger stages of these plants typically offer greater amounts of protein and are easier to digest, so once exiting the den black bears often head right for such areas. In the East, river and creek bottoms, as well as swamps, often green up first with skunk cabbage, green briar, pokeberry, wild strawberry, squawroot, and various grasses—all prime areas in which to locate spring bears.

While as much as 80 percent of the bear's diet is composed of plant matter, it will rarely pass up an opportunity to dine on meat, either carrion from a winter kill or fresh prey. In Newfoundland it's estimated that up to 20 percent of caribou calves are killed annually by black bears, and elsewhere bears are known to prey on other young ungulates during the spring period, such as moose and elk calves and deer fawns. Meat, including fish such as salmon in Alaska and along the west coast of Canada and spawning white suckers in the upper Midwest, is particularly important to bears in the spring because it gives an immediate protein boost and supplements the primary diet of carbohydrates obtained from grasses and emerging forest plants. Black bears are often spotted scouring saltwater beaches along the west coast in search of fish, shellfish, and other foods that are washed onshore. The same is true along rivers, streams, and lakes.

As spring turns into summer, more carbohydrate-rich foods become available, and the black bear immediately takes advantage of it all. South-facing slopes and meadow bottoms begin to dry out, and as these locales lose their succulent spring grasses, bears look to other areas, perhaps moving to north-facing slopes where spring green-up has been delayed and tender sprouts are still available.

In the spring, south-facing slopes often green up first. These areas attract grazing bears that are hungry after their winter naps.

By midsummer and into early fall, a smorgasbord of wild berries becomes available; find the berries and you'll find black bears. Depending on location, the list includes blueberries, huckleberries, June berries, pin cherries, black cherries, pokeberries, blackberries, sarsaparilla berries, squawroot fruits, raspberries, dewberries, wild strawberries, currents, gooseberries, cranberries, and bilberries, to name but a few. These foods are not universally available, but each region has its indigenous berry and fruit crops. Rest assured that bears will seek them out.

In the Southwest, prickly pear is a favorite food, in parts of the Pacific Northwest and northern California it's patches of manzanita (a small apple-like fruit), in northern New England they like blueberries and other brambles, and in the southern Appalachians there are holly berries, black cherries, dogwood berries, wild persimmons, and sassafras. Black bears will also seek out beehives for honey and bees and root around in anthills or for grubs and snails. They also eat small rodents such as mice and dine on frogs, salamanders, turtles, and crayfish when near water.

The hunter who has invested the time to locate these foods has a major advantage over those who haven't. The time of year when most of these foods become available, generally sometime in August and September, is the peak feeding season for black bears. During a good year, when these foods are readily available, an adult black bear might forage sixteen hours or more a day and consume anywhere from 50,000 to 200,000 berries, remaining in an area until the supply is exhausted. Luckily for hunters, the fall season usually coincides with this feeding frenzy.

This is also the time of year when agricultural crops are coming on. Cornfields draw bears like a magnet, as do apple or other fruit orchards. These areas should be investigated thoroughly for bear activity. A single bear can lay down a relatively

Bears will spend long hours in search of food.

large area of corn in no time, and the evidence is usually quite apparent. In orchards, it's not uncommon for bears to actually climb trees to reach the fruit, breaking limbs and branches in the process. The ground is apt to be littered with half-eaten pieces of fruit, and scat will be everywhere.

As the various berry crops begin to diminish in quantity, and agricultural crops have been harvested for the year, black bears start to concentrate on various hard mast. In the East, this means nuts such as acorns (preferably from white oaks) but also beech-nuts, hickory, and hazelnuts. In the high country of the West these nuts are often from whitebark and piñon pines. These as-sorted nuts offer the most digestible and concentrated source of energy and are also high in protein, which helps lay on the fat for winter.

During this fall feeding spree the average black bear will put on several pounds a day, eating its fill, defecating, resting for brief periods in between, and eating again. This process continues until food becomes scarce. When scouting bear country, also keep an eye out for dug-up anthills, overturned rocks, rotten logs, stumps and trees that have been torn apart, even broken branches on hardwoods.

Food is the dominant factor in a black bear's movements. If you're hunting in unfamiliar territory, state game biologists can provide information on preferred foods in a given area, even where they might be found. One of the best things a hunter can do is make contacts and start asking questions. The names of re-gional or district wildlife biologists, and related contact informa-tion, are easy to obtain through state fish and game agencies; some are even posted on their websites.

If you intend to hunt in national forests, state parks, or on other public ground, district rangers and wardens can also be of great help. Many national forest and state park headquarters even

Bears often feed through the night. This young bear was caught on the author's motion detection camera at 3:30 AM.

publish informative fact sheets about common wildlife in their area, including what they like to eat and where those foods are found. Even if such materials aren't available, personnel who work and live in the vicinity can certainly point you in the right direction.

Local gun shops are another good source of information. Many proprietors of these establishments are hunters themselves and are quite knowledgeable about the habits of local game animals. The same is true of taxidermists. I once asked a Montana taxidermist about possible bear activity in his area. He pointed out the fact that he had noticed a bumper crop of huckleberries on a particular ridge while bird hunting a few days earlier, and suggested it would be as good a place as any to start. I spent two days glassing and working the area, and although I didn't kill anything on that trip I did spot two nice bears.

In agricultural areas, farmers and orchard owners can be immensely helpful, providing information on whether they have experienced any crop damage or seen any bears. Local information is always best. Have they seen any bear sign in the area? If so, where? Was it recently, a week ago, perhaps a month? Are there any general areas where bears have been seen year to year? Ask about areas where local foods might be found.

Not all local contacts will be able to indicate exactly where a bear lives, or even whether one has been seen in the area lately. But if they know where there is a beechnut grove or where blueberries or other foods are abundant, chances are any bears in the area will be aware of it too, and you now have a place to start looking. You may even luck into an actual bear sighting. A bear can be observed in a particular area one day and literally be miles away the next. Then again, it may still be there. You never know.

Asking local farmers and wildlife biologists where they've been seeing bears may cut down on your scouting time. Water sources are always a good place to start. (USFWS)

Every bit of information obtained, every possibility, every hunch, is worth investigating, but this takes time and effort, and lots of it.

It's a common misconception among novice bear hunters that the time and effort necessary for scouting bears is the same as for deer. This is far from true. For one thing, deer are less mobile than bears, and their daily movements are much more predictable because they are generally traveling between bedding and foraging areas. The bear is more of a rambler, and its movements and whereabouts are difficult to predict.

Deer are also more reluctant to leave their home range unless forced to do so. Not so with black bears. They go where their noses lead them, even miles outside their home territory. Fortunately, these movements are nearly always tied to food or the hunt for food. So when scouting bear country, whether new or familiar, locating food sources and knowing when they'll be most productive is often more important than actually seeing bears. Find the food, and you'll eventually find the bear.

BEAR SCAT

The droppings left by a bear are generally called scat. Scat is a valuable sign of a bear having been in the area, but it's much more than that, too. A close examination can tell the hunter what the bear has been consuming, and therefore where to look for further activity or the actual presence of bears. Scat color and texture can indicate, to a degree, when the bear passed through the area, and a concentration of scat within a small area may indicate a bedding spot. Scat tells us a great deal; we just have to read the signs.

When firm, black bear scat is tubular and averages between 1¼ and 2 inches in diameter. In general, it's a fair assumption that larger scat indicates a larger bear, but it's not an absolute, particularly when it comes to adult bears. While a mature male or female certainly has the capacity to deposit more waste, younger bears are ferocious feeders and can, at times, leave as much scat as an adult. The intestine and rectum of a three-year-old black bear is not really much smaller than that of a five- or six-year-old.

So while it's encouraging to see large piles of scat when you're out scouting, it's by no means a guarantee that you're onto mature adults. There is no way to accurately ascertain if the bear weighs 175 pounds or 300 pounds just by looking at its scat.

Since black bears are omnivorous, their scat is often as varied as their diet, particularly in terms of consistency, color, and shape. Once leaving the den each spring, the black bear typically dines on lots of grass. As discussed earlier, this is largely because grasses are among the first forms of vegetation to emerge beneath melting snow, but also because grasses are tender, succulent, easy to digest, and help recondition the stomach and intestinal tract after hibernation. Scat from grass and other succulents is generally blackish or dark greenish-brown, apt to be full of grass-like fibers, and generally firm, compact, and uniform in shape. Depending on freshness, scat left from plant materials will sometimes have an odor similar to the inside of a silo or hay loft.

Bear scat is a useful scouting tool.

This is in stark and obvious contrast to scat derived from a diet of berries and nuts. When black bears get into a berry patch they typically gorge themselves. Much like they do in humans, wild berries have a laxative effect on bears, and the subsequent scat is often runny and loose in texture. Rain can break down berry scat and make it appear watery or juice-stained.

Such scat is often close in color to the berries in it. Blueberry scat tends to have a blue or purple tint, raspberry and chokecherry scat is somewhat reddish, and scat from sarsaparilla is generally reddish to dark purple. Bears barely chew berries, but rather swallow them whole, letting the stomach muscles break the pulp off the seed. The stomach often does a poor job of it, however, and many berries, particular those not yet ripe, come out almost whole or as a mixture of pulp and seed. Berries that are ripe generally depart the bear looking more like seeds than actual berries, but seeds are almost always present.

This is important to keep in mind because all berry seeds don't look the same, and detecting what fruit is being consumed in a particular area can lead to bears. For example, blueberry seeds are rather small, roundish, and look like sand, while seeds of wild sarsaparilla are flatter and half-mooned shaped. Seeds from chokecherry and wild grape are larger, often cream colored.

Wild berries also contain a lot of water, and when they are the primary food source, bears drink very little. They'll still utilize it, but water is less important at this time of year.

Scat composed of acorns, beechnuts, and other hard mast is firm, and often has bits and pieces of the nut in it. Scat derived from apples will contain apple seeds, which are easy to recognize. Bears living where corn or other agricultural grains are readily available typically deposit scat that has complete kernels throughout because digestive juices simply penetrate the kernels and grains to remove nutrients, leaving the husks. Such scat often takes on the color and texture of the primary grain consumed. There is almost a pleasant odor emanating from scat derived from fruit and hard mast, much like the food source itself.

Scat from meat, fish, and various protein-rich foods is generally black, often with hair or small bones and scales present. It can be firm or soft, almost human-like, and nearly always has an unpleasant smell.

Studying scat may also give the hunter an indication of how long ago the bear passed through the area. Despite its firmness or consistency, all bear scat contains a certain amount of liquid when it leaves the body. This liquid evaporates at a rate dependent on a variety of factors: original moisture content from food sources, time of year, weather conditions. Scat from various berries has the highest liquid content, so it generally dries at a slower rate.

Of course, it all depends on where the scat is located, in full sun or shade, for example. But unless the weather is cold, it

The color and consistency of scat may help you find natural feeding areas nearby.

generally takes three or four days for berry scat to completely dehydrate. If a scat composed of berries appears moist throughout, there is a good chance the bear recently passed through. If it appears dry on the surface but retains moisture inside, it may be a day or so old. If the scat is dry throughout, it's at least several days old. This doesn't necessarily mean the bear has left the immediate area, though, especially if berries are still available in the area.

Bear scat from grasses, meat, and hard mast generally contains less water, so it generally begins to dry out and break down more quickly. Again, many variables contribute to this, but under average conditions such scat is noticeably dry within a day or so and dry throughout in two days. When bear scat is completely dry and dehydrated it has a tendency to turn hard, almost brittle, similar to that of a dog. It's often blackish in color, although coloring may vary depending on the original food source.

There are other ways to tell freshness, however. One is to turn the scat over. If the vegetation beneath it is fresh and green, a bear may still be close, or at least in the area. If the vegetation is yellowish, it is probably at least a day old. Also, look for insects and flies. Both are attracted to fresh scat, although less so as it dries.

Grizzly scat can resemble that of a black bear, and hunters scouting areas where these bears coexist need to remember this. Both bears eat the same basic foods in season when occupying the same home range, and telling the difference in scats can be difficult even under laboratory conditions. Size is not a factor here, since a lot of grizzly scat is less than two inches in diameter and roughly the same size as black bear scat. At times, grizzly scat can be more ball-like and have a slight smell of pepper, but even that is not a guarantee. When exploring country where both bears are apt to be found, move with caution, particularly around animal kills and other food sources.

A couple of other facts about scat should be mentioned here. Along with winter dens, black bears also have favorite summer bedding sites within their home ranges. While it's not uncommon for bears to lie down and take a nap just about anywhere, especially after heavy feeding, they often return to favorite bed sites for long daytime sleeps. It's not unusual to discover lots of scat in these areas, and it's often concentrated because bears tend to defecate in one or two general areas once they rouse themselves and begin activity.

Concentrations of scat may also be present near feeding areas. Move cautiously, though, since a bear may be near. Also, only examine scat using a twig or stick, never with bare hands. While bear scat has no diseases or parasites that transmit to humans, handling scat can leave human scent, and since bears often return to an established area to defecate while feeding or sleeping in a certain locale, that scent can betray your presence.

TRACKS

Tracks are another reliable sign that black bears have passed through an area. Despite their bulky size, wide body, and weight, black bears walk flat-footed, or plantigrade, like humans. The bottoms of their feet are well padded with soft skin tissue and hair, making tracks extremely difficult to find in forest habitat. In general, especially for the untrained eye, the best places to look for tracks include anywhere there is soft mud and sand: along the edges of swamps and the banks of creeks, rivers, and lake shores, even along gravel roads after a rain. Search slowly and meticulously, preferably on foot.

When tracks are found, it should be possible to distinguish front and hind paws. Tracks can also indicate whether a bear is walking or running, whether it's a male or female, even how big the bear is and whether it's worth pursuing. Carry a small tape measure afield to get an accurate reading of track size.

Let's look at the hind feet first. The five toes are slightly separated by hair, and the smallest inner toe is to the side and rear of the others. In other words, the "big" toe is the outer toe. The hind foot has a palm pad and well-defined heel pad that are longer than they are wide. The rear pads on an average adult will run five to six inches long, measuring just the pads and not the toes. Rear pads are widest just behind the toes, tapering to the heel pad. The heel pad often shows up in tracks.

In soft mud or sand, the overall size of the hind foot is always longer than it is wide, generally measuring 6 to 7¾ inches long by 3½ to 5½ inches wide, although they can run larger. Any black bear with a rear foot measurement greater than eight inches is a real trophy. The hind foot track of younger black bear will run proportionately smaller. The hind foot also has an uncanny resemblance to a bare human foot. The claws are short and don't

Tracks are often visible in bear country. Shape will indicate whether it's a front or rear print.

always show up in the track. When they do, they often appear as small indentations close to the toes.

The front feet differ in several notable ways. They look squarer and less human. More specifically, both pads—and the whole foot—are wider than they are long. On an adult black bear the forefoot is about 3¾ to just over 5½ inches wide by 4½ to 6¼ inches back to front. The front tracks made by a male are nearly always larger than females, and in general, any front track at least four inches across is that of a boar that will probably dress better than 250 pounds. Older males, those over seven years, rarely have front feet measuring smaller than 4½ inches, and any front foot track measuring five to six inches across is huge.

The heel pads on the front feet are generally quite small. It is often covered with hair and seldom shows up in a track. Also, the front claws are longer than the rear claws, and under ideal tracking conditions the tips are often visible a bit farther out from the toes.

Given that female tracks are nearly always smaller than males of the same age, track measurements can provide hunters with a lot of information. Tracks can even be used to estimate the approximate square size of the bear hide.

To use the front track measurements to determine the squared hide size, simply measure the width of the front footprint in inches, convert it to feet, then add one foot, carefully considering any slippage in mud or soft sand that may make the track appear larger than it really is. This provides a solid estimate of what the bear hide will square. If, for example, the track measures three inches, the bear will square around four feet (3 inches = 3 feet + 1 foot, or 4 feet). If the track measures four inches it should square around five feet and so on.

Any black bear that squares five to six feet is worth pursuing in my book, and anything larger, between six and seven feet, is a

Measuring the front paw can help determine the "square" size of the bear's pelt.

real trophy, perhaps even a record-book contender, since the assumption that black bear with big feet have big heads generally holds true.

This method of squaring the hide should not be confused with actually measuring the overall length of the bear. Many guides and outfitters simply measure the bear from tip of nose to tip of tail to get the length. If the bear happens to measure five feet this way, it's simply called a five-footer. The proper position in which to measure a bear this way is with it resting belly down and all four legs stretched outward in spread-eagle fashion with the hide still attached. This is a great way to measure a bear because it proves the truth length. The hide can also be measured in the same fashion once it has been removed, taking care not to

*To "square" the bear, add length and width measurements
and then divide by two.*

over-stretch it, although measuring before skinning gives a more
accurate length.

Here again, any black bear measuring five to six feet from
nose to tail is a good one, and anything six to seven feet is a prize
in most areas. Bears measuring better than 6½ feet this way will
probably have a skull measurement close to record-book minimums, depending on the method of take.

Like all bears, black bears are pacers, moving both legs on
one side of the body at the same time. In other words, they alter-
nate both right limbs and then both left limbs as they walk. This
alternating gait is why bear tracks can double register—with the
rear foot typically overstepping slightly in front of, or on top of,
the front foot—depending on ground conditions and how fast

the bear is moving. The two-on-two pattern generally indicates a faster gait.

The average walking stride of a black bear is somewhere between eighteen and twenty-eight inches, measured from one rear track to the next rear track. The longer the stride between the two tracks, the larger the bear. When running, the stride can vary anywhere from twenty-five inches to as much as fifty-five inches, and each group of four tracks can range from forty-five to as much as sixty-seven inches. The actual distance depends on speed: the greater the distance, the faster the bear is traveling. It's helpful to know this if you happen to spook a bear or when tracking with dogs.

It is also interesting to note the direction in which the tracks are pointing. Generally, black bears walk pigeon-toed (toes inward). This often seems less apparent with cubs, immature adults, and even some adults, especially sows, although all black bears have this same basic characteristic to some degree. The exception is with older, bigger boars. A heavy boar walks with a seemingly ponderous effort, and at times will leave severely pigeon-toed tracks. So if you find a good-sized track that noticeably points inward, chances are it belongs to a hefty boar.

In areas where black and grizzly bears occupy the same territory, it's important to recognize the difference between the two tracks, particularly since grizzlies are a protected species across much of their remaining range. Size alone is not a good indication, since young grizzlies and some adult black bears will have feet of similar size.

There are, however, more reliable methods. One is to measure the toe and nail, or claw, lengths. On nearly all black bears, the nails are shorter than a grizzly's, and the nails of a black bear are shorter than corresponding toe lengths. The nails on a grizzly are as long or longer than its toes. Also, the black bear often has noticeable spaces between the toes, while a grizzly's are closed, appearing bunched together.

Another solid indicator is that the toes of a black bear are arranged in more of an arc. A grizzly's toes appear in more of a straight line. Place a straight twig or string across the top of the pad on the track, and the difference will become more obvious. If the toes appear arched, and if the smaller inner toe is below, or mostly below, the line, it is probably a black bear track. If the toes are straight across and the inner toe is above the line, chances are high that it's a grizzly. (See the end of this chapter for additional information.)

BEAR TREES

The bear is largely a creature of the forest, and it's rarely found where trees aren't present, although in the far north more and more black bears are being observed on the open barrens. For the most part, however, black bears love trees. In a nutshell, trees provide shelter and food, are used to mark territory and leave scent, and even provide a place to sleep or nap. The bases of hollow trees are even used by some bears for winter dens. Various markings and damage to trees are clear indications that bears use an area regularly.

There are three basic types of bear trees. Both sexes are known to strip bark from spruce, pine, fir, and other conifers, as well as cedars and small redwoods, among others, to get at the cambium and sap beneath. This is generally done in the spring when sap is running full and other foods are scarce. At times, the damage from such activity can be quite severe, completely girdling the trunk and causing the tree to die. In most cases, this stripping occurs low to the ground; it may appear as if the bark has been peeled or shredded.

Both deciduous and coniferous trees are used for scratching and as scent posts. While sitting on spring and fall bait stands, I've witnessed both sexes and all ages enjoying a good scratch now and then. Perhaps they're just easing an itch, but the practice seems particularly prevalent among adults during late spring and early summer, the shedding and mating seasons. To rub, a bear stands erect on its hind legs and may rock back and forth, up and down, or both. The upper sides near the backbone, along the spine, the back of the neck, and the head seem to be the most popular areas to rub.

Within their home range, the same tree or trees may be used over and over again for years, and the bark on such trees can appear worn, or even polished. Rubs are most often found along well-used trails. It's not uncommon to find scratches or bite marks on rub trees, as well as hair stuck in the sap or in bark bordering the rub. Bear hair is rather fine and long, somewhat like human hair; it's not short and coarse like moose or deer hair.

Evidently, many rub trees also serve as scent posts, primarily used by adult males. Standing on its hind legs, a boar will stretch as high as possible and, just before or after rubbing, reach up to bite or claw the tree, leaving noticeable markings. On some trees, bite and claws marks may appear barked or scabbed over, indicating long-term use of the same tree. It is not known for certain whether this practice is an attempt to specifically mark territory, deposit scent, or indicate size and dominance. Very possibly, it's all three.

Many fresh markings and rubs seem to correspond with the mating season, from May through July, and the claw and bite marks are high off the ground, often too high to have been made by cubs or sub-adults. From a hunting perspective, it's not a bad idea to make note of any fresh bite marks, since their height off the ground is generally indicative of the length of the bear that

Black bears use trees for various purposes: to seek food, rest, rub, or mark territory.

made them. Note, too, that bears will rub, scratch, and bite telephone poles, high tension poles along power lines, and even wooden sign posts. These are all good areas to investigate in bear country, since the ground around them is often soft, making it easy to locate tracks.

Trees are also used for food and rest. Black bears are great climbers, and their claw marks can easily be seen in smooth-skinned trees such as beech, maple, birch, and various other hard- and soft-mast species. They can even be seen in pine, apple, oak, various firs, black cherry, aspen, and mountain ash, among others. Just about any tree that buds and offers some kind of fruit or nut is apt to be utilized. Recently broken limbs, limbs that appear as if they suffered through an ice storm, and clusters of limbs pulled together are possible signs of bear activity.

Bears seem to like large trees with forks in the main trunk or large branches that allow them to sit or lie down while munching. Even small fruit trees and berry bushes are susceptible. If a tree, shrub, or bush is too small and fragile to climb, limbs or even entire trunks will be bent over or broken to reach food. The damage is often quite easy to spot.

Black bears will also, at times, construct what are called "bear nests." These consist of branches broken off and roughly pulled together to form a nest-like area. It's not known whether these are actually built to serve as beds, although bears have been observed resting and napping in them. They may be pulled together to make food more obtainable as the bear lays back and enjoys the feast.

OTHER THINGS TO LOOK FOR IN BEAR COUNTRY

Food, tracks, scat, and rub trees are all important signs to look for when scouting. Most are relatively easy to find and reveal a great deal. However, there are also other things to watch for.

Trails are a prime example. Trails around bait sites are fairly common, and these areas are useful in learning how to recognize what a bear trail looks like. Usually, several trails lead to and from a bait area, and although it's not set in stone, bears seem to have their favorite way in and out, depending on the wind and other factors. This is especially true of large boars.

Other good areas in which to find trails include possible feeding and watering grounds. Like all game, bears use traditional routes to move between such areas. Game trails used by deer, moose, and other hoofed game are often used by bears, too, since there is always the possibility of running across a sick or dead animal. Wallows are good areas, as well. Look for a small spring or pool in a creek where bears might go to cool off. They'll often use the same trails to reach these areas over time, and nearby vegetation may show evidence of the mud and water bears shake off when they leave the water.

As a general rule, heavily-used bear trails traverse the thickest cover possible, often literally tunneling through brush, thickets, and tall grass right up to their destination, be it a food or water source or a place to bed or cool down. These critters prefer cover and use it whenever possible. On average, bear trails vary from about nine or ten inches to as much as fifteen or sixteen inches wide, and in thick, overhanging cover are usually about three feet high.

On well-used bear trails grass and other vegetation will be noticeably flattened or compressed, almost like a well-worn path. This is especially true where bears place their feet, as they generally place their feet in the same spot each time they use a trail. Even a bear using a trail for the first time will place its feet in the same spot as other bears before it. This is helpful to know, whether hunting bears or exploring around a bait site, since the matting can indicate which direction the bear is traveling. Spots worn down to bare earth often reveal clear tracks.

While exploring a bear trail, be sure to look for hair. The bordering brush often acts like a comb pulling out hair as the bear passes. Scat is sometimes present, too.

Digs are something else to look for. As noted earlier, black bears love a tasty meal of ants, grubs, beetles, bees, and other insects and their larvae, and these foods are often found in decaying stumps, in and beneath rotting logs and rocks, and in the ground. Black bears will excavate these sites, ripping stumps and logs apart, overturning rocks, and demolishing anthills and beehives. Where acorns, beechnuts, and other nuts have fallen to the ground and lay covered with leaves, bears will often rake away the cover.

Besides occasionally resting in trees, black bears also have day beds on the ground. These beds are often found at the base of trees or along a fallen tree. They are about the same size as deer beds, although they often appear more circular. Beds are frequently found around bait sites, since these critters seem to enjoy lying down while eating. It's not uncommon for bears to sneak into a bait, grab something to eat, and return to the thickets to lay down and consume it. In areas where natural foods are plentiful bears will often travel a short way off, lie down in a comfortable spot, and rest as they digest the contents of their full stomachs.

BIG BEAR OR SMALL BEAR

One of the biggest challenges facing the novice bear hunter is distinguishing a small bear from a big one in the field before the trigger is pulled or the arrow flies. Their thick fur makes all bears, evens cubs and yearlings, appear bigger than they really are.

There are, however, some reliable indicators that can be used afield to determine young bears from older bears, and therefore small bears from large. These aren't always precise, but they do hold true much of the time and are pretty much all we have to go by. As author Tom Brakefield states in *Hunting Big-Game Trophies*, because they lack horns or antlers, when judging bears "we must instead rely on a lot of assumption and interpretations based on indirect comparisons." Older bears are always bigger bears, both in terms of weight and skull size, the measurement used for record keeping.

Let's start with the head. Unlike the brown or grizzly bear, the snout and head profile of the black bear is fairly straight, almost dog-like, rather than dished. In general, the skull bone is long and wide across the forehead, averaging around 11½ inches long by 6½ to 7 inches wide. As a black bear ages, the skull increases in size, so older, bigger bears will have larger skulls. The skull also seems to flatten in the forehead area as it widens, especially on boars, which nearly always have a proportionately larger skull than sows.

Cubs are usually easy to identify in the field, particularly if the mother is close by.

Due to the increased skull width, the snout may appear fat or pug-like, even short in older males. Overall length is also greater in males than females most of the time. Because scoring practices take in only two measurements, length plus width, boars tend to dominate the record books. Cubs and sows always seem to have a face profile that is narrower and longer than boars, and this characteristic may also be discernable in some young males.

As the skull grows and widens in later years, the ears tend to move outward—more to the side of the head than on top. The ears also become shorter and more rounded, again more so on males than females. These telltale indicators occur more on much older bears, but close scrutiny of the head often reveals other signs of maturity. Simply put, they *look* older. And because older means bigger, those are the ones we want as trophies.

Now let's consider the body, starting with the legs. As a bear grows and ages it naturally gets bigger. But the belly of an older

Careful study of body shape and head size will help you estimate a bear's trophy caliber.

and bigger bear seems to hang lower, making the legs appear shorter and stouter. The legs on a young bear often seem long and spindly, and the bottom of the belly is high off the ground. A lanky-looking bruin is most likely a sow, often with cubs, or a yearling. Older bears seem to have more muscle and bulk, with bodies that look more developed, or just bigger, even in spring.

Ironically, an older, bigger-bodied bear can actually appear to have a small head due to its sheer size. A bear that appears big-headed in relation to its body is most likely a juvenile or young adult that hasn't fully developed.

It is also possible to estimate a bear's size and whether it's worth taking by the way it moves. Young and middle-aged black bears move with an almost springy gait, with little movement in the buttocks, as if they are full of life and energy. This is especially true with cubs, yearlings, and sub-adults. Like human tots and teenagers, they seem to have energy to burn. Older and bigger bears, on the other hand, move at a slower pace, with mincing steps and a ponderous, rolling, duck-waddle-type stride. This is especially apparent in the oldest and biggest boars. They look old and move accordingly.

MALE OR FEMALE

Even more difficult than judging size is determining sex. Unlike deer, elk, and moose, bears lack the headgear that clearly indicates gender. But determining sex is important because females are protected in some jurisdictions, primarily during spring hunting season. Some hunters also prefer harvesting males because they are bigger and offer a better chance at a trophy.

Here again, there are some telltale signs that suggest sex. The easiest and surest, of course, is to spot an adult with cubs. This is obviously a female. Boars have nothing to do with cubs or yearlings, are never in their company, and are often con-

In most states and provinces, killing sows with cubs is prohibited.

fronted by sows when they do get too close. Likewise, a bear traveling or feeding alone is most likely a boar. If you're sitting on a bait or glassing a berry patch where a sow and her cubs are feeding and another adult of about the same size, or larger, comes in alone, it's likely a boar. If the cubs hightail it for cover or climb a tree and the sow become highly defensive, agitated, or quickly departs, you can almost count on the intruder being male.

In general, boars are solitary and highly protective of feeding areas. So if you happen to be glassing a bear at long range and see another lone bear come in and there's a confrontation, chances are good that both are males.

Females generally have little to do with boars except during the breeding season. But not all females travel with cubs. Some sows may be traveling alone because they're too immature to breed or because their cubs may have died young. In these situations, sexing is more problematic. During the spring and early summer, however, a boar's penis and testicles are often clearly visible between the rear legs. A tuft of long pointed hair hanging down from the belly marks the spot.

When two adult bears are seen together from late May into July, the larger one is most likely the male. This is especially true if the larger bear is following the smaller one. In this situation, the male often makes soft grunt-like sounds, especially when the female is actually in heat.

Determining the sex of two adults in the fall is a bit more challenging. By then the boar's testicles have receded into the abdomen, and the penis and scrotum are hidden by hair. Still, look at the belly hair, which is often much longer on females than males in the fall. At times, it can be mistaken for a penis between the rear legs, so look carefully. Size is often a better indicator. Males are nearly always bigger than females, with larger heads

Boars usually travel alone, but they may be in the company of sows during the spring mating season.

and longer bodies. And as noted earlier, lanky-looking bears, if not cubs or yearlings, are most likely sows. Boars also have broader, more heavily muscled shoulders.

In some cases, the remoteness of an area, or lack of it, can suggest sex as well as size. Boars especially prefer remote locales, while smaller bears and sows with cubs are generally found closer to roads, farms, ranches, and populated areas. Pest bears, such as those found around camps, for example, are likely sows with young. Boars are also more aggressive, confrontational, and protective of feeding sites. They'll usually stand their ground, while females will almost always give way, often departing the area as soon as a boar is detected. This is particularly true if she is accompanied by cubs.

A TROPHY IS A TROPHY

The word "trophy" means different things to different hunters. The first black bear I harvested thirty years ago barely tipped the scales at 130 pounds. It wasn't a monster by any means, but I considered it a trophy then, and it will always have special meaning for me. Today, however, I wouldn't give a bear this size a second look.

In most cases, a bear is considered a trophy based on weight, measurements (total length or squared), and skull size. It's all relative and subjective, but for the record books an official trophy is determined by skull size, using the greatest length added to the greatest width to get the total. There are no penalties as with antlered and horned game, because there are only two measurements. The correct total length is taken in a straight line from the occipital region (the rounded edges of the spinal cord hole at the rear of the skull) to the premaxillary bone and incisor teeth. Width is the greatest distance across the zygomatic arches of the cheek area. Skull measurements are made with the lower jaw removed, since it is not part of the actual skull, and these are recorded in sixteenths of an inch because the simple measurements allow such accuracy. (Most other game animals are measured to eighths of an inch.)

Measurements are taken with all flesh, cartilage, and membrane removed, after a sixty-day drying period that starts at time of death. If the skull has been boiled, frozen, or stored in any environment other than normal atmospheric conditions, an additional sixty-day drying period, starting at the time of boiling or thawing, is required for it to be official.

OFFICIAL RECORD-BOOK MINIMUMS FOR BLACK BEAR

Boone & Crockett (All-Time/Awards)	Pope & Young (Bow)	Longhunter Society (Blackpowder)	Safari Club (Bow/Rifle)
21/20	18	18	16/18

Bears are also considered trophies once they reach a certain length when measured from tip of nose to tip of tail. As indicated previously, measuring this way gives the true length, but has no official designation. For some hunters, a black bear is considered a trophy when it exceeds five and a half feet, but six feet is a better minimum, since black bears up to six feet aren't uncommon in many areas. In my book, any bear with a true length greater than six feet is a very good specimen, and anything over six and a half feet is a real doozy. Bears of this size are often boars, and their skulls should be dried and scored for possible record-book contention.

Other hunters prefer to determine trophy-size by squaring. Because two measurements are used, length plus width (the total of which is then divided by two), trophy minimums are generally considered to be slightly less. If a bear squares five and a half to six feet, it's a very good bear, something to extremely proud of. It's also worth scoring the skull, particularly if it's a boar. Anything squaring over six feet is a true trophy. Again, score the skull.

When it comes to weight, any female from 200 up to 220 pounds or so is a very respectable black bear and should be considered a trophy. Anything heavier isn't even debatable. For boars, minimum trophy weight is around 250 pounds, and anything up to and over 300 is a real prize, perhaps even the bear of a lifetime. Of course, all of this is relative to the specific area, quality of habitat, hunting pressure, "average" size of bear taken in various locales, and other factors. And in the end, other than the official minimums for various record books, it all boils down to personal opinion.

For some hunters, whether a bear qualifies as a trophy even depends on color. Unless the pelt is extremely thin and badly rubbed, it's a rare day when I don't consider a color-phase bear a trophy, regardless of weight or measurements. They are truly magnificent and a welcome addition to any trophy room. Even

Trophy value is subjective, but color-phase bears like this one are always prized.

with black-phase bears, whether the pelt is thin or rubbed can determine its trophy status. Thinning usually occurs first around the eyes, toes, and underbelly, starting around June. If possible, scrutinize those areas carefully while assessing an animal through binoculars, in a treestand over bait, or with a spotting scope.

KNOW YOUR BEAR

The grizzly bear, *Ursus arctos horribilis*, once roamed over much of the western United States, from the Great Plains to California and from central Mexico north through western Canada into Alaska. It's believed that the grizzly population ran as high as 50,000 or so. Due to habitat loss and indiscriminate killing, however, the great bear all but disappeared from this vast area by the early 1900s. The last known grizzly bear in Utah was killed in 1923, and the last verified death in the Bitterroot Mountains of central Idaho and western Montana occurred in 1932. In 1975, the grizzly was listed as a threatened species by the U.S. Fish and Wildlife Service (FWS) under the Endangered Species Act of 1973. (Obviously, this doesn't apply to Canada.)

As early as 1982, a federal grizzly bear plan by the FWS called for studies to locate suitable habitat for the recovery of the grizzly bear. By 1991, an Interagency Grizzly Bear Committee had been formed, which authorized the FWS to pursue grizzly bear recovery with the ultimate long-term goal of removing the animal from the threatened list in the lower forty-eight states.

Today, the grizzly bear has been reintroduced to several ecosystems in the western United States, and is believed to occupy about 2 percent of its historical range outside of Canada and Alaska. Less than a dozen are believed to live in the northern Cascades of Washington State, perhaps 25 in the Selkirks of northeastern Washington and northern Idaho, 20 to 50 in the Cabinet-Yaak area of northern Idaho and western Montana, some 350 in the northwestern mountains of Montana, and perhaps 250 in and around Yellowstone National Park.

It's imperative that all bear hunters in these areas know the difference between black bears and grizzlies, because these bears coexist in each recovery zone except Yellowstone Park. Killing a grizzly in the lower forty-eight states is a federal and state offense that can bring criminal and civil penalties up to $50,000 and a year in jail.

In 2002, Montana began requiring that all hunters complete a bear identification test in order to purchase a black bear license. Hunters can receive the test by writing Montana Department of Fish, Wildlife and Parks–Bear Test, 1420 East Sixth

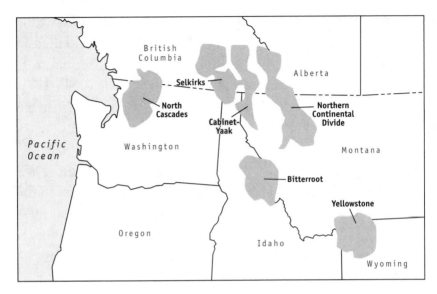

Grizzly bear recovery zones in the Lower 48 States (courtesy of the Center for Wildlife Information).

Avenue, P.O. Box 200701, Helena, MT 59620. Or they can receive training, take the test, and become immediately certified online at fwp.state.mt.us. All Montana hunters must pass the test by April 15 for the spring hunting season or August 15 for the fall season. Other states are considering similar requirements.

The following features can be used to identify grizzly bears and black bears. (Special thanks to the Center for Wildlife Information for this list. Contact them at CWI, P.O. Box 8289, Missoula, MT 59807; 406-523-7750; www.bebearaware.org.)

GRIZZLY BEAR

- Color varies from blonde to black. Often medium to dark brown legs, hump, and underside, with light-tipped (grizzled) head, face, and upper body.

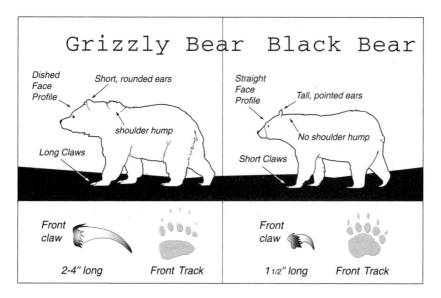

Grizzly Bear and black bear identification (courtesy of the Center for Wildlife Information).

- Weight averages 500 pounds for males and 350 for females. Males may weigh up to 800 pounds.
- Height is 3½ to 4 feet at the shoulder on all fours, 6 to 7 feet when standing.
- Shoulder hump is distinctive.
- Rump is lower than shoulder hump.
- Face profile is dished rather than straight.
- Ears are round and proportionately small.
- Front claws are 2 to 4 inches long, slightly curved, and not good for climbing. They're usually visible in tracks.

BLACK BEAR

- Color is primarily black, but also brown, blonde, and cinnamon. Light-brown snout. White markings on chest.

- Weight averages 200 to 250 pounds for males, with some up to 500 pounds. Females average under 200 pounds.
- Height is 2½ to 3 feet at the shoulder on all fours, up to 5 or 6 feet when standing.
- No shoulder hump.
- Rump is higher than front shoulders.
- Face profile is straight.
- Ears may be long and prominent.
- Front claws are less than 2 inches long, dark colored, sharp, curved, and good for climbing. Claws do not always show up in tracks.

Chapter

3

HUNTING METHODS

With the exception of whitetail deer, the black bear is perhaps the most regulated big game animal on the continent. There are laws on the books regulating just about every imaginable aspect of hunting this animal. There are a couple of reasons for this.

Except for some national parks, refuges, and other federal lands in the United States and Canada, the responsibility for all wildlife management falls under state, provincial, and territorial wildlife agencies. In general, these agencies decide when or even if hunting seasons will be held, bag limits, which areas will be open to hunting, whether special permits will be required, legal hunting means, and which sex may be legally harvested.

In Wisconsin, for example, it's mandated that baits be placed in a hole no more than two feet square, while in other states and provinces it's legal to use exposed bait. In some areas, baiting or the use of hounds is legal only in certain areas, or at certain times of year, and may be completely prohibited. In Arkansas, baiting is allowed only on private property, but its use is prohibited completely in states like California and Colorado. In New Mexico hounds can be used only in certain areas, in Alaska just in the fall, but in Maine they can be used throughout the state.

While sows accompanied by cubs are almost universally protected, in some areas it's legal to harvest sows traveling alone or when not accompanied by cubs. In New Jersey, which held its first bear hunt in more than thirty years in the fall of 2003, both the use of bait and hounds is prohibited. In Wyoming, there are female mortality quotas throughout the state, and once that quota is achieved the area is closed to further bear hunting.

In most states and provinces bear licenses are available over the counter or through licensed outfitters and guides, while in others licenses are available only through a special lottery or draw. New Jersey only issued licenses to hunters that passed a spe-

Black bears can be hunted using several methods and a variety of weapons.

cial bear hunting course. Only a general hunting license is required to hunt black bears in some states, in others a special license or tag must be purchased separately. Throughout Canada, a special bear license or tag is the general rule. In a number of states, license requirements for residents differ from non-resident requirements.

This complex set of rules and regulations is most often based on in-depth field research and other factors such as game populations, or desired populations for available habitat. In some parts of Alaska, which has one of the largest black bear populations on the continent, hunters may harvest up to three black bears annually. The legal limit in parts of Idaho and Washington is also more than one bear annually; the same goes for many Canadian provinces and territories.

Where bears are less numerous or habitat is not as abundant, the bag limit is generally one bear annually. In some jurisdictions, primarily in Canada, residents may legally harvest more bears than nonresidents. These bag limits are generally intended to keep bear populations at healthy levels, and hunting has become a viable management tool. Extensive research has given wildlife biologists and managers a good idea of how many bears a particular habitat and range can sustain.

Unfortunately, in a growing number of cases, how black bears are hunted has been mandated by public sentiment through state ballot initiatives. In 1992, Colorado voters passed Amendment 10, which did away with bear hunting during the spring and prohibited the use of bait and hounds. In 1994, Oregon voters passed an initiative prohibiting the hunting of bears with hounds, as did Massachusetts and Washington in 1996. That same year additional but unsuccessful attempts to ban spring hunting or hunting with hounds or bait were also made in Idaho and Michigan. This year, voters in Maine will decide on an initiative to ban hunting with hounds and bait, as well as the trapping of bears.

No matter what is printed in the press or shown on television, these ballot initiatives are nothing more than well-funded efforts by anti-hunting groups to do away with the legal hunting and harvest of bears. Similar initiatives pertaining to all hunting are sure to follow.

These initiatives have nothing to do with sound wildlife management practices, or even what is best for wildlife in the long term. While it may seem to make little sense that killing an animal is in its best interest, the truth is, man is continually encroaching on bear habitat. The use of bait or hounds for bear hunting are viable management tools in a world where more and more bear habitat is being taken away while bear populations continue to increase. Whether or not hunting should be allowed is a decision best made by trained wildlife professionals who know the local situation.

In 1999, Ontario did away with its spring hunting season under orders from its Natural Resources Ministry, not based on sound management or because of a lack of bears, but because of emotional rhetoric from animal rights groups. The closure proved so unpopular in central and northern parts of the province, which are largely rural, that it sparked calls to split Ontario into two provinces, north and south. This hasn't happened, but a proposal to extend the fall season, which now starts in mid-August and runs to the end of October, was passed in some areas.

In every case where ballot initiatives have been passed or decisions made to halt the hunting of bears by politicians or judges, a viable management tool has been taken away from trained wildlife biologists. As a result, bear populations are increasing in some areas, with an unhealthy long-term scenario developing for bears and humans alike. Human-bear encounters have become more

Hunting behind hounds isn't legal every-where, but it's an exciting way to take bears.

common, even in suburban areas. This can mean bears must be trapped and physically removed, or in some cases, even killed in the name of public safety. Ironic. When a population increases beyond the carrying capacity of a particular habitat, it could eventually collapse.

There are also great variations from state to state and province to province on mandatory check-ins for harvested black bears. Presently, nearly all the states where bear hunting is legal require some kind of reporting. In some jurisdictions where this is requested or required, special tags are supplied with hunting licenses. Depending on the type of hunt, identifying body parts are left with the guide or outfitter who turns them in or they are turned in directly by the hunter.

Bear hunting is currently allowed in eleven Canadian provinces and twenty-eight states. The following table shows the various states and provinces where bears can be hunted, along with legal methods of doing so. Where the use of bait or hounds is prohibited, spot-and-stalk tactics may be used. And in states or provinces where the limit is two bears, only one may be taken in each season (spring and fall), although in Idaho it is legal to take both bears in the spring.

It should be noted that in some areas, such as Alberta, residents can legally harvest up to four bears annually, but non-resident Canadians may only take one bear in certain areas. Guides and outfitters may also limit their clients to just one bear per season, or year, to conserve numbers in their area.

Considering the amazing array of regulations pertaining to bear hunting across North America, all hunters should make themselves aware of local rules by contacting a guide, outfitter, or the appropriate wildlife agency.

LEGAL HUNTING METHODS

State/Province	Legal with Bait	Legal with Hounds	Annual Limit
Alaska	yes	yes	1–3
Arizona	no	yes	1
Arkansas	yes	no	1
California	no	yes	1
Colorado	no	no	1
Georgia	no	yes	1
Idaho	yes	yes	2+
Maine	yes	yes	1
Massachusetts	no	no	1
Michigan	yes	yes	1
Minnesota	yes	no	1
Montana	no	no	2
New Hampshire	yes	yes	1
New Jersey	no	no	1
New Mexico	no	yes	1
New York	no	no	1
North Carolina	no	yes	1
Oregon	no	no	2
Pennsylvania	no	no	1
South Carolina	no	yes	1
Tennessee	no	yes	1
Utah	yes	yes	1
Vermont	no	yes	1
Virginia	no	yes	1
Washington	no	no	1–2
West Virginia	no	yes	1
Wisconsin	yes	yes	1
Wyoming	yes	no	2
Alberta	yes	yes	4
British Columbia	no	yes	4
Manitoba	yes	no	2

State/Province	Legal with Bait	Legal with Hounds	Annual Limit
New Brunswick	yes	no	1
Northwest Territories	no	no	2+
Nova Scotia	yes	no	1
Ontario	yes	yes	1+
Quebec	yes	no	4
Saskatchewan	yes	yes	2
Yukon Territory	no	no	1+

BAITING

Baiting is without question the most controversial method of hunting black bears. Of the twenty-eight states that currently allow bear hunting, only ten allow baiting: Alaska, Arkansas, Idaho, Maine, Michigan, Minnesota, New Hampshire, Utah, Wisconsin, and Wyoming. In Canada, baiting is permitted in eight provinces: Alberta, Saskatchewan, Manitoba, Ontario, Quebec, New Brunswick, Nova Scotia, and Newfoundland. It's also al-

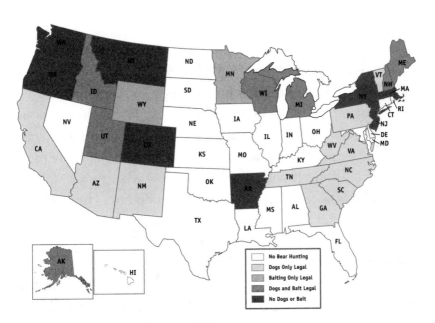

Hunting over bait or with hounds, United States.

Legend:
- No Bear Hunting
- Dogs Only Legal
- Baiting Only Legal
- Dogs and Bait Legal
- No Dogs or Bait

Hunting over bait or with hounds, Canada

lowed in Labrador, but technically Labrador is part of Newfoundland and governed from St. John's, the provincial capital.

Those opposed to its practice claim it's unethical, inhumane, or unsporting—often all three. Such statements are generally made by people opposed to all types of hunting or by those who haven't done it and really don't know what they're talking about. The truth about baiting is just the opposite. Hunting over bait is done at close range, often at distances under fifty or sixty feet. This makes proper shot placement for a quick, clean kill much easier than it is for spot-and-stalk hunting, where two-hundred-yard shots aren't uncommon. Such long shots invariably lead to more wounded game, while close-range shots from gun or bow are much more likely to dispatch animals humanely.

Hunting over bait also allows the hunter to study his target closely before shooting. In addition to assessing overall size and pelt condition, the two most important trophy criteria, the close-up view makes it easier to determine sex. This is extremely important in areas where sows are protected, since it's difficult to sex black bears at great distances.

Seen in this light, baiting is really one of the most sportsmanlike methods for killing these animals. As for being ethical, ethics are a personal thing, something instilled in each of us from youth. Unfortunately, the politically-correct ethics of a few are being legislated into laws that govern us all. It may go against someone else's grain to hunt bears over bait, but for the reasons enumerated above it doesn't go against mine.

One thing there is no debate about, however, is that baiting is an extremely productive way to hunt bears. In states and provinces where a variety of methods are legal, bait hunters almost universally produce the largest annual percentage of harvested bears. This is partly due to the fact that baiting can be done, with some degree of success, by just about anyone. Also, only a few hunters have the time to train, and the room to house, a pack of hounds, and hound hunts are generally the most expensive outfitted hunts. Perhaps the biggest reason, though, is that black bears are eating machines. When done properly, particularly in areas with a healthy population, attracting bears to a bait isn't overly difficult.

Baiting can be so productive that in situations where wildlife managers see a need to reduce the bear harvest it's often the first method to go. In some states where bear populations are just holding their own or are rather small, baiting isn't allowed because it would result in too high a harvest. Where baiting is prohibited in the West, it's often because grizzly bears would also be attracted to bait sites.

This bear was taken over bait during the fall. The pelt is full and in fine shape, typical for late-season fur.

Although baiting is highly effective, it still requires some skill to do it well. There are times when success can be had by simply placing some food anywhere bears are known to frequent, but for consistent success it's much more involved. Where they're placed, the types of foods used, the quantity, when stations are actually baited on a daily basis, and how bait is placed in relation to stands are all key factors. While bears are certainly aggressive feeders, they aren't stupid and can often be unpredictable.

WHERE TO PLACE BAIT

Perhaps the most important aspect is where to place the bait. Black bears roam over a home range that can cover many miles, and within that range there is at least one core area where they spend much of their time. These core areas provide the best food and water sources and good cover. Such areas can be difficult to locate, but if you scout thoroughly using the information from the previous chapter, you should be able to zero in on high-use areas. Even if a bait is established outside a core area, it can still work well if it's in the home range because bears are great roamers and can be drawn in from long distances by a variety of scents.

The bait station must also be placed in a spot where bears feel comfortable moving around during shooting hours. There must be ample cover right up to and around the bait, and the area should be well away from human activity, which always makes bears more wary. Generally speaking, bears are nocturnal, preferring to feed late and early in the day and under the cover of darkness, but they always break the rules. This is especially true in the spring, before mating season, when their full concentration is on assuaging their hunger and again in the fall when they are storing fat for the winter.

One of my biggest black bears was taken just before noon on a bright, sunny day, and I've taken several others at midday and during the early afternoon under full sun. Bears that only come to a bait after dark, or at times when a hunter can't take advantage, may have a reliable source of food elsewhere. But it may also mean that the bait is located in the wrong place, using the wrong foods, or too close to human activity. The time at which we provide bait each day and the lack of sufficient cover may also play a role.

There are a lot of variables, but proper cover and placement are paramount, not only for the bear but from a hunting perspective, as well. Start by looking for sources of natural food. During the spring season, bears graze extensively on grass and greens. They also eat roots, insects, wander along rivers and lakes for spawning fish, and take advantage of winter-kill deer or other carcasses. In summer and early fall, berry patches and areas where hard mast are plentiful will always attract bears.

The best bait stations are often established before hunting season. A patch of wild cherries, an apple orchard, or oak grove might not offer any food during the summer, but they are still good bait sites because bears will check them out when these foods do become available. Because baits are started early, areas that offer the potential for food can be just as good as areas that actually have food. Find the natural food or potential food sites and you should find bears. It is often that simple.

Once a reliable food source has been located, confirm bear activity by looking for sign, particularly scat, scratchings, and torn and battered brambles. If signs are present, seek out the thickest cover and set up along the edge or actually within it. The hunter will have to determine which spot is best depending on the circumstances, but there are some basic pros and cons to consider. Bait stations along the edge of cover are often best because they offer better visibility, and because bears will usually enter an area from only one or two directions and from the thickest cover. This allows the hunter to place his stand in a spot that takes full advantage of the most likely routes.

On the other hand, baits more in the open, such as in sparse timber, can be hit later in the day, particularly by wary bears or by bears with some prior experience with baits and humans.

Bait stations completely surrounded by thick cover are often hit earlier in the day—perhaps after sunrise, at noon, or midafter-

The location of natural food sources and available cover will help you determine good spots for baiting.

noon—because the bear feels more secure. Also, the bear is likely to come more frequently, maybe even on a more regular schedule depending on your baiting schedule, and chances are it will stay on the bait longer during each visit. This translates into more sightings, more time to look the animal over, and more time to line up the best shot. Baits in heavy cover are also less likely to be discovered by other hunters.

The downside to setting up in such heavy cover is that although bears often use one or two main trails, heavy cover may allow them to approach the bait from any direction, depending on the wind, which makes stand placement much more important. And stands in heavy cover usually have to be located closer to the bait due to restricted visibility, and as a general rule, the closer the stand to the bait, the less the chance for success.

Again, each situation is different, and the hunter will have to make the final decision based on the specific circumstances. But it's important to weigh all aspects carefully before placement.

Water is also a major factor, particularly in the spring when bears require lots of water to rehydrate. Grasses and greens, roots, and other foods commonly eaten in spring are not overly moist, so more water is needed to digest these foods. Water is less important in the fall when berries and brambles are available, but as a general rule, locating bait near a reliable water source is a good idea since bears typically drink at least once a day. Look closely for possible sites along the edge of rivers, creeks, and smaller seepages, as well as in the bottoms where bears travel. These areas often provide lots of cover and are natural travel corridors. Keep in mind, too, that bears generally drink after eating, so thick cover in these areas may also be used for resting places. Ideally, the bait station will be close to a reliable water source and near natural foods, so bears don't have to travel far to drink.

Scouting thoroughly often results in a large bear like this one.

FOODS FOR BAITING

Black bears are opportunists that will consume just about anything, but there are still some factors to consider when choosing the type of bait to use, especially for large boars and adults. The type of food should depend on time of year and the location of the bait site. Although bears are fast and powerful, they aren't the most skilled predators compared to other carnivores. Despite this ineptitude, black bears do love meat. In the spring, meat is always a good choice because it provides a quick protein boost after hibernation. During late summer and fall when hard and soft mast are available, it's one of the few foods hunters can use that will almost assuredly draw bears away from natural foods.

Around water, fish or fish parts are another good bait. Bears love fish, although it spoils fairly quickly. Fresh meat added to fish can be an excellent combination, and once bears find a reliable source they'll return to it again and again. This is particularly true for large boars. The combination of foods will also hold bears on or near a bait for the longest period of time.

While bears often eat carrion, they seem to prefer fresh meat (beef parts) loaded with fat and fresh fish over rotten, foul-smelling, maggot-infested meat and fish. Fresh chicken is a good bait, too, but beef is invariably the way to go because it's the one food we can supply that actually resembles, and smells like, wild meat. More than once I've been on a stand where sour-smelling chicken and rancid meat and fish were used, only to see bears come in, sniff, and move on without eating or concentrate on other foods placed at the site.

Use a lot of meat, especially when trying to draw in large boars. They can eat huge amounts on each visit. Prior to the baiting season, I routinely make contact with butcher shops and slaughterhouses in my area to ask for beef scraps. Even if I have to pay a little for the trouble, I ask that they place the meat in fifty- to seventy-five-pound boxes, and freeze it. If that isn't possible, I use five-gallon pails with covers, and then freeze it myself. I keep it frozen until baiting time, and then use one box when establishing the bait and one box each time I add bait after it initially gets hit.

Check with local farmers that raise cattle, too. A cow will die occasionally and the farmer may be anxious to get rid of it. Of course, you will need a way to transport such a large carcass to the site, but it's worth the effort because it makes excellent bear bait. Where legal, the same is true of beaver carcasses. Bears absolutely love them, and they are worth their weight in gold. If you know a beaver trapper or two, ask them to save the carcasses. They can be used whole or cut in half, but keep them frozen until baiting time.

I also use meat to create scent trails when first establishing a bait site. A slab of meat or fat, a beaver carcass, or fish tied to a rope can be dragged through an area along an indirect route leading to the bait site. I like to work routes through ravines, along brooks, and in areas of thick cover that bears are most likely to use naturally, making each trail roughly a half-mile long. The idea is to intercept a bear that might be traveling through. Once he hits the scent trail, odds are high that he'll come to the actual bait.

Scent trails work extremely well, especially when setting up a new station, and two or three coming in from different directions are even better. Once the bear finds the bait and knows it is a reliable food source, he'll often stay in the vicinity and return on a regular schedule, and scent trails will no longer be necessary.

Bears also have a sweet tooth, and even with meat, something sweet works wonders. My wife, Diane, makes several cases of homemade strawberry, raspberry, and blueberry jam each summer and fall when the berries become available, and she would probably divorce me if she discovered how many I sneak out for bear bait each fall. It works well anytime, but especially when you start baiting and bait in the fall. At some retail outlets and grocery stores, preserves can be purchased by the case in one- or two-pound jars at a responsible price, and outdated jars can sometimes be purchased for little to nothing. Bears find it irresistible, even when wild berries are available. It's particularly effective when baits are placed in areas where wild berries are scarce.

Here again, don't be skimpy with it. If possible, use at least a couple of pounds of the stuff each time you bait. Put some in the bait hole or bucket and smear some on surrounding trees at knee and chest level, which allows wind currents to carry the scent.

Donuts and other sweets work well, too. Sweet breads containing honey and molasses and donuts covered with sugar, filled with jelly preserves, or glazed with sugar are all excellent. Search out bakeries in your area and ask for any old donuts, breads, and muffins. Outdated sweets not sold at stores are generally returned to commercial bakeries for credit. They have to get rid of this stuff, and if it's not free it will certainly be cheap. I'm lucky enough to live near a large bakery where I can fill up the back of my pickup for about ten dollars.

Molasses also works extremely well. It has a strong, sweet smell that can be detected for miles when the wind is right, and when mixed with dry dog food it's irresistible to bears. It can be purchased at feed stores in five-gallon buckets for around fifteen

Bears love to eat almost anything, so don't be afraid to experiment with different foods for bait.

dollars. I generally put one or two gallons on my baits each time out, especially if the bait is getting hit daily. Honey works well, too, although it can be a bit costly. Again, it has a sweet smell that carries extremely well on the wind, so I always make sure to smear it around the bait area at various levels after adding it to the bait itself.

Honey works so well that my good friend and outfitter Joe Cabral, who operates commercial bear camps in Maine and Idaho, uses it as an attractant in situations where bears are not showing regularly or are being otherwise difficult. Joe creates what he calls a "honey burn." When the hunter is taken into a bait, Joe or one of his guides pours about a quarter to half a cup of honey into a metal coffee can. Using a tin of Sterno or small Bernz-O-Matic propane torch, they heat the honey until it boils then burns and smolders, forming a thick smoke. Once the honey is completely gone, the guide departs, taking the can with him, but the honey aroma lingers in the air.

Joe claims that bears can smell it for miles and find it irresistible, and I have no doubts that he is correct. I recently hunted with Joe in Idaho in an area where all signs pointed to a large boar feeding nearby, but it wouldn't come in regardless of the hour I took to the stand. On the fourth afternoon, totally frustrated, we tried a honey burn. Two hours after Joe departed I took a 280-pound male.

Various other foods can also be used. Canned dog food, the cheapest kind available, works well. A can or two added to the bait itself each time out and some smeared around to release the smell should do the trick. As mentioned, dry dog food is good stuff, too, especially when mixed with molasses or other sweet liquids. When honey or molasses isn't available, Karo syrup and commercially made maple syrup, which are both cheap and readily available in grocery stores, are good substitutes.

Dry dog food actually has some advantages over breads and pastries in that it's relatively cheap and won't mold or spoil in hot or wet weather conditions. Be generous in the amount offered, providing at least three or four well-mixed pounds each time you bait.

Grains such as oats, barley, and corn are effective, too. These grains are readily available at feed stores in fifty-pound bags, aren't expensive, and complement meat and sweets, particularly when mixed with molasses and other sweet liquids, or when mixed with water and allowed to ferment. Dr. Ken Nordberg, a noted bear expert, hunter, and writer, suggests mixing ten gallons of corn, oats, wheat, or barley with five gallons of water and ten pounds of sugar in a clean fifty-five-gallon drum. Simply stir it, set it in the sun to warm, and wait a week or two. I've tried it, and it works well. Blue-Seal also sells a commercial wildlife mixture of coarse cracked corn, flaked corn, oats, barley, soybean meal, molasses, and soybean oil that works extremely well.

In agricultural areas, sweet corn, apples, and other fruits make good baits because bears are used to eating them. They work on bears in wilderness areas and away from farms and orchards, but it may take a little longer for bears to come in. The best apples are obtained locally, either at an orchard or in someone's yard, since apples purchased at the grocery store are hard, firm, and have been washed, handled, and shipped in packaging. "Drops," apples that have ripened and fallen to the ground, make excellent baits because they're soft, sometimes even partially decayed or starting to rot, and have a strong, sweet, almost fermented odor.

When using corn, leave it on the cob with the husks still intact. Use as much as ten or twenty pounds of produce to start with, reducing the amount by about half once the bait becomes active.

When attempting to bait large black bears, particularly large boars in areas where other hunters might be baiting, use a variety of foods and large quantities. Boars quickly lose interest if only one type of food is available. So two desirable foods are better than one, three are better than two, and so on. You simply can't offer too much variety, not only because bears are accustomed to eating a wide range of foods, but also because multiple foods emit more bear-attracting smells. Bears will hit such baits on a more regular schedule, often daily, and they'll stay at the site for longer periods each time they visit.

Large boars can eat up to forty or fifty pounds of food a day, if it's available. Too many outfitters I've hunted with over the years, however, don't provide enough bait, using the bare minimum to lure a bear in and keep it at the site long enough for a shot. Of course, they're usually running a string of several dozen baits, which can be expensive to maintain. In most cases, a small amount of bait still works because each site has about the same amount of food, and hunting outfits often work in exclusive areas where their baits have no competition. Once the food is gone, the bear moves on, often to one of the other baits in the area.

I once hunted with an outfitter in New Brunswick who ran a string of three baits along a four- or five-mile stretch of old logging road. The only bears hitting the baits at the time were a sow and two cubs. The hunter on the first bait would see them around two in the afternoon, the hunter on the second bait about two hours later, and the last bait would get hit just before dark. We had a good idea they were the same trio because of a white mark on the chest of the mother and because one of the cubs walked with a noticeable limp.

The baits were probably placed too close together anyway, but the point is that it takes a lot of bait to feed a sow and two cubs, even more to feed a boar, and these bears were obviously hitting all the baits daily. The sow was off limits, anyway, but had one of the baits offered a large quantity of food it would have been the primary feeding station, and there is a good chance the sow would have remained in that area instead of traveling so much.

Most hunters don't have exclusive rights to a given area, so when competing with other bait stations, it's a good idea to work hard on variety and quantity. Bears are hungry when they come

to a bait. If sufficient food isn't available, they'll eat what is there and quickly move on, perhaps to a natural food source or someone else's bait. If they can find a greater source of food on a regular basis elsewhere, your baits become less productive. Give them enough to keep them

Pile on the food, because bears can eat incredible quantities in one sitting.

interested and they won't work as hard to search out other sources of food.

I start off with a forty or fifty pounds of bait, checking every other day or so until the bait is hit. Once bears arrive, I start baiting every day and try to maintain at least fifty pounds of food at a site, which I consider the minimum if a large boar is the primary visitor. If the available sign indicates that more than one bear is using the site, 75 to 150 pounds may be necessary to keep them coming back regularly. Bears generally eat less in spring than fall, so these amounts can be adjusted according to what is going on at the time.

A large amount of bait also keeps a bear comfortable at a bait site, more at ease with its surroundings. When this happens a bear is apt to sit down on its haunches. I've even seen them lay down to enjoy the feast, perfectly content. Whatever the case, the longer a bear is on a bait, the more forgiving it is of sounds you might make while preparing to shoot, and the more time you'll have to get off a good shot. Everything becomes easier, but this can only happen if enough food is at hand to hold the bear.

Grease left over from frying bacon, sausage, and other meats, and old cooking oils used for frying chicken, even French-fried potatoes, can be used to add extra incentive. (Even whole strips of bacon can be used as an attractant.) I routinely collect these items in tin coffee cans or gallon jugs that I set aside for baiting season. Area restaurants use a lot of cooking oil and may have old grease on hand that they're happy to get rid of, often free of charge. Grease from meats congeals into a handy paste-like form when cooled, and although cooling oils remain in liquid form, they have strong, salty odors that carry well.

I use both grease and oils as attractants, but in different ways. I include some bacon or sausage grease, as well as a few strips of fried bacon, when establishing a new bait station because it seems to work quickly, and I always add more when planning to sit because once bears know it is there they keep coming back. The grease can easily be dabbed on trees and bushes in the area, and the bacon strips hung on branches near the bait where it can be seen from the stand, again at different heights. Place dabs of grease low, perhaps a foot or two off the forest floor, to provide scent close to the ground, and add some five or six feet off the ground, again for scent, but also because a bear reaching up for tidbits provides a good target.

Although used cooking oils can also be added directly to the bait, I prefer to pour or brush it on surrounding cover, as well. I know one guide who applies grease and oil to the bark of trees using a paintbrush. If a rotten stump or decaying log is nearby, touch it up on each visit. The oil soaks into the wood, helping to permeate the area with scent, and bears will literally tear the stump or log apart to get to the grease. Anything that keeps them on the site for as long as possible is a good thing.

I always apply a generous quantity on the ground completely surrounding the bait, covering as much of the immediate area as possible. When a bear comes in and begins to forage he will walk through it, picking it up on his pads. When he departs, he leaves a nice scent trail for any other bears in the area.

Attractants are always a plus when a bait is first placed, but they are equally important throughout the hunting season because they keep working even after the bait itself has been depleted. Anise, vanilla, and licorice flavorings seem to work well in the spring and in areas where hard masts are a primary food source, while strawberry, raspberry, and other fruit flavorings are great attractants in early fall in areas where these foods are available, or even where they aren't. Bears will rarely pass up an opportunity to investigate a potential feast of berries. Several guides I know even use a hickory smoke scent that seems to work well.

While these scents can be dabbed on surrounding cover like cooking oil, the key is to disperse the smell throughout the area and to make it last as long as possible. Some guides soak strips of cloth (flannel and terrycloth both absorb well) in a small container of scent. Each strip is about an inch or so wide and five inches long. The strips are then dropped over branches near the bait station, and replaced as necessary.

You can also put several of these strips in a small plastic container pierced with holes and dangle it from a branch. Several 35mm film canisters with scent-soaked cotton balls inside work well, although the amount of scent that can be used is limited— and I like lots of scent. In small plastic containers, the material stays wet and lasts longer because it's protected from sun and rain, but the container does restrict the flow of the scent to a degree. I've found that strips dropped over twigs work far better. Just remember to keep them fresh.

Commercial scents designed for black bear are also available, and most work extremely well. They can be purchased in convenient four- to thirty-two-ounce containers, but also by the half-gallon or gallon. Some are even available in a gel that's easy to dab on trees and surrounding cover. One of the best is Bear Scents, out of Lake Mills, Wisconsin. According to owner Brad Hering, the scents are made to the fullest strength possible, primarily derived from foods bears naturally seek in the wilds or

Adding scent to a bait station will help you get a bear's attention.

A guide adds a scent rag to a bait area. Various commercial scents are available if you don't want to create your own.

from other potent aromas that will bring bears in from miles away.

Bear Scents is available in anise, apple, bacon, wild berry, loganberry, raspberry, watermelon, wild cherry, honey, hickory smoke, shell-fish, blueberry, corn, straw-berry, and other aromas. The scents are even available in a spray bottle for easy application around bait areas, and for creating scent trails. Bear Scents offers a handy eight-pound scent ball that acts much the same way. It's designed to slowly dissolve, dripping fresh scent to the ground and emitting scent into the air in the process. It comes wrapped in netting that includes a loop for easy hanging.

Bear Bait from Wildlife Buffet is also an effective commercial product. It comes in two-pound tubes of paste that can be cut and quickly dispersed around baits and along trails. It holds up very well in all kinds of weather conditions and has an aroma attractive to bears. Another good product is a series of lures from Nature's Own out of Manteno, Illinois. Their Bear Call Lure has a shellfish essence, while their Bear Focus Lure is a paste with the aroma of chicken or bacon. It can be used to create a honey burn of sorts. They also offer a sweet-smelling formula called Bear Focus Call.

Even though baiting may be a legal practice where you are hunting, certain types of baits may not be allowed. In some western states and provinces, meat may not be used because it may attract grizzly bears. Honey is prohibited in a few states, too, so always check the local regulations before preparing bait.

BAIT CONTAINERS

How bait can be offered may also be regulated. A few jurisdictions require that bait be placed in the ground and covered with logs, small rocks, and other debris. But most states and provinces don't have such restrictions. Again, check the regulations.

The first time I ever saw bait in the ground was on a hunt in Newfoundland. At the time, I wasn't sure whether I liked the technique or not, although I did bring home a nice boar. My reservations were based on the idea that bait below ground level, particularly when covered, wouldn't give off enough scent, but this is not necessarily the case. The key to this method is to provide plenty of additional scent above ground, particularly along trails leading to the site. Once bears are attracted to the bait station, they will find the food and dispense with the logs and brush in short order.

One advantage to this type of bait hole is that it keeps other marauding critters like the fox, coyote, wolf, and bobcat, even birds, from stealing the bait. In areas where these and other robbers are prevalent, placing bait in holes is often the best way to go. Bait placed in covered holes also has a tendency to keep bears on the site longer, since they have to remove the covering themselves. I have seen hole baits used in Ontario, Manitoba, Maine, and Idaho, all with success.

And it really doesn't have to be much of a hole. While I've seen guides painstakingly dig a hole a couple feet deep by several feet wide, natural holes and cavities at the bases of trees, hollowed-out trees, and other small depressions can be used. One of my best bait sites ever was a pine tree about three feet at the butt that had rotted from the inside out and fallen to the ground. The base was completely hollow and made a perfect cubbyhole for the bait. After dumping the bait, I would use a stick to push the bait into the hollow cavity a couple of feet so a bear would have to work to reach it. The nearby stump was a perfect spot for dispensing grease and other attractants.

Baits can also be placed in covered plastic buckets and suspended four or five feet off the ground. At that height, odors are better dispersed, and the bears will have to stretch to reach the bait, perhaps even standing in the process. This opens up the vitals area and may offer a better shot. At this height the bucket is also out of reach of other animals that might visit the site.

Five-gallon buckets are about the right size. They hold sufficient amounts of bait, have covers to keep out the rain, and are durable. I use them to carry my bait into an area, simply dumping the contents and taking the empty bucket out when I go. If the bait bucket is gone or demolished when I get there, which is sometimes the case, I have another bucket ready to go. The bait bucket should have several half-inch holes drilled into the sides, with perhaps another dozen

Many guides and outfitters prefer to establish baits on the ground, near logs or stumps, where the bait will work its way into the ground. A pail also works well.

Suspending a five-gallon bucket off the ground keeps the bait out of reach of other animals and helps spread scent.

or so in the bottom. Not only does this allow scent to escape, but it also lets water, grease, or oil drain to the ground.

When securing the bucket to a tree, I generally use wire the size of a coat hanger. It's easy to twist and strong enough to hold the bucket off the ground, yet light enough to be pulled to the ground by the bear. Once it's on the ground, he'll spend some additional time working to remove the cover. Again, this is all intended to keep the bear interested, occupied, and on the site. So I don't secure the bucket too tightly, just enough to keep it in place.

Canvas bags and onion sacks work well, too. They are porous enough to let scent escape and actually soak up liquids, which helps keep the scent active for long periods of times. Bags can be suspended over a limb five to six feet of the ground using twine; almost like a food cache, but lower and more accessible.

Many guides and outfitters use fifty-five-gallon drums as bait containers. They hold a lot of food, are very durable, and when laid on their sides make a nice deep hole or cavity that a bear almost has to climb into to get the bait. They are also too heavy to be carried off. The only problem is they can be difficult to lug them into a bait sight, because the best sites are in, or near, dense cover and at least a hundred yards off any road or

Fifty-five-gallon drums make good bait stations. They hold a lot of food and often keep bears on the bait longer. Notice the scent bag in the tree on the left.

trail. I like to place mine even farther back in the woods, perhaps a quarter-mile or so in, since it reduces the chances of human interference. The farther away it is from roads and trails, the more comfortable a bear feels coming into it, especially during daylight hours.

Some folks simply dump food on the ground next to the base of a tree, stump, or log. This works, but it's easier for other animals and birds to steal the bait. Over time, as the site becomes increasingly active, visiting bears will grub around and dig up the ground, creating a depression in which bait can be placed.

BAIT SCHEDULES

Just as important as location and types of food and scents is the baiting schedule. While black bears are opportunists, they are also creatures of habit. Many return to known food sources and use the same trails and dens for years. The same is true for bait sites. Not only will bears often return to established bait areas year after year if not killed, but they can be conditioned, to a certain degree, to visit within a set timeframe.

Most domestic animals are fed around the same time each day. Ever notice how excited they get, even following you around as you prepare the food and take it to their feeding station? They've grown accustomed to being fed at the same time each day; bears react the same way. Once they become comfortable with a reliable food source they'll hang around the general area and pattern their movements according to yours, just like deer that feel pressured.

Many times while checking highly active baits with outfitters, a bear has entered the scene within thirty minutes to an hour of when the truck door slammed. I shot one of my largest bears before the guide even started the engine on his way out. It's not just coincidence; it happens too often. Bears that are being regularly fed become conditioned to expect food at a certain time of day, and may even wait patiently nearby for it to arrive. Once they know food is there, they wait to make sure all is safe, and then make their move. It may take as little as ten to thirty minutes, depending on the bear.

Boars, for example, are generally more cautious and take their jolly old time. Females traveling alone are apt to move in quickly, hoping to feed and depart before a boar arrives. Cubs and sub-adults, low members in the hierarchy, are often the first to arrive. If you're on stand, keep an eye on them. If they act nervous, picking up their heads to gaze into the woods at every little sound, chances are they're expecting a larger visitor. If they suddenly stop feeding, look into the woods, and then sneak away quickly, that larger visitor is probably very close. Notice which way they depart, too. The new bear will most likely come in from the opposite direction, giving you a slight edge.

Not all bears come to a bait quickly, however. But if they have been regularly hitting a bait site, chances are high they're still conditioned to having the food available. Some bears make regular rounds within their core areas, and some might like to stop and rest. It may simply take them longer to arrive, but when they do, the food better be there.

Once you've started a baiting schedule, one of the worst things you can do is deviate from it. A bear might forage fifteen to twenty hours each day depending on time of year and prevailing conditions. Contrary to common belief, hunting in the morning and at midday can be just as productive as late afternoon. The hour at which a bait site is actually baited makes little difference. The bear will adjust to your schedule as long as you are consistent.

If you have more free time to hunt early in the day, baiting in the morning could prove best. If you want to hunt the afternoon hours, consider putting out bait around noon. Don't bait too late in the day, though, because the largest boars are likely to come in under the cover of darkness, well after shooting hours. I like to bait no later than one or two o'clock in the afternoon, often earlier. During the spring and early fall, this gives a bear several hours to come in before dark—plenty of time. Every situation is different, and the best time to bait your site may have to be determined by trial and error. But once you establish a schedule, stick to it.

TREESTANDS

When, where, and how stands are erected is also important. Scouting for home range and core areas should begin well before the hunting season. If you're planning a fall hunt, spring and summer explorations aren't too early. For spring hunts, start looking for potential hunting sites the prior summer and fall. I look for sign and potential bait sites each time I'm afield, no matter why I'm out there. There are no guarantees with scouting, since bears move around so much and their presence month to month, even week to week, depends on natural food availability, but early scouting should at least provide you with some idea about where bears should be when hunting season arrives.

Once a site has been selected, I like to set up treestands, and particularly ground blinds, at least a week before I start laying out bait. In some cases, limbs must be removed to create a shooting lane, and erecting a stand creates a disturbance. Put it up before a bear starts using the area on a regular basis. Doing this also provides some time for any bears in the area to get used to the stand before baiting begins.

Deciding whether to use a treestand or a ground blind, and where to place a stand, will depend on the circumstances. For example, is there a tree within the desired shooting range that will safely accommodate a stand? Some thought should also be given to where a stand might best take advantage of prevailing wind currents. If hunting along a ridge, which is often the case in mountainous terrain, remember that thermals drop toward evening and rise during the day.

Stands that face into the wind, or at least crosswind, are often the best, particularly if more than one hunter will be using a stand. But to be honest, I give wind very

Put some thought into where you hang your stands, and make sure they're comfortable.

Assemble stands well before the season to allow bears to become accustomed to them.

little thought on sites I bait and hunt myself. Just like any animal, a black bear will eventually grow accustomed to your scent in the area. The bear may even associate your scent with food, particularly if you've been careful to maintain a strict baiting schedule. By the time hunting season rolls around, your scent should have no effect on the bear's movements or willingness to come to a bait.

Each time a site is baited, human scent will be left behind, and in time a bear will ignore your scent. He will know what trail you use, perhaps even how long you spend baiting each site and how long ago it was baited. Here again, not deviating from the baiting ritual is important. Use the same trail in and out of a bait area, and try to spend the same amount of time there each day while baiting. Get in and out as quickly as possible.

Bears are quite intelligent, and they will probably notice that a stand has been established. They may even investigate it. A few years ago I tried an experiment when I started baiting a particular site. I left an old shirt or jacket in the stand, just to see what might happen. To my surprise, nothing happened. Once the bait was initially hit, it was hit regularly, and I took a nice boar there. That bear had become accustomed to my scent being in the area, so it didn't really matter.

When planning spring hunts in areas where mosquitoes and blackflies can be bothersome, I even spray on insect repellent when baiting, adding a little around my stand to help condition the bear. Use the same insect repellent before the season, while baiting, and while hunting. While human activity around a bait should be minimized whenever possible, it's impossible to completely hide human scent while baiting and hunting, so don't try. It makes much more sense to condition the bear to its presence. This is why I always bait my own sites, and allow no one else to do it.

The situation is more complicated for guides and outfitters, who must bring bears in to stands used by different hunters. Although wind and rain will, in time, dilute multiple human scents, they have a tendency to make a bear nervous, perhaps even causing it to alter its schedule. While most guides and outfitters do a good job of placing stands and bait to minimize human scent, even preventing hunters from approaching the bait in some cases, human odor can be a factor on stands that are used by different hunters over the course of a season.

Some hunters uses scent-eliminating activated carbon clothing to mitigate the problem. I have my doubts about how effective the stuff really is, but it can't hurt. Before

Human scent isn't much of a problem around stands if you've been maintaining your own bait stations prior to hunting season.

each day of hunting I do try to minimize scent by using little or no pungent deodorants, soaps, or shampoos and by keeping my hunting clothes free of household or camp odors. I generally stow my clothes in a plastic bag filled with fir needles or other natural materials.

When hunting over commercial baits, I do like the scent-neutralizing sprays, soaps, deodorants, and shampoos, such as those from Hunter's Specialties and Wildlife Research Center. These products generally contain an ingredient called Tri-closan, which is highly effective and known to kill bacteria that cause odor. But on my personal stands, I rarely bother with these.

Generally, I like the sun at my back whenever possible during the most productive shooting hours. Any tree used for a stand should also provide some background camouflage. Background cover will help break up your outline if the bear looks your way. The stand location should also provide a clear shot to the bait, and have a decent view of the area surrounding it.

Most shots with rifles and muzzleloaders over bait are under fifty yards, sometimes well under, and at this range stands ten to twelve feet above the ground are high enough that the bear won't take notice most of the time. This is also high enough to help carry away human scent and provide a proper trajectory into the kill zone. When using bows and handguns, closer shots are the rule, so stands should be a bit higher, up to fifteen feet.

Most guides and outfitters establish their stands close to the bait. They aren't always familiar with a client's shooting ability, especially with the excitement of actually seeing a bear up close. Short shots minimize the chance of wounding an animal.

Because I have seen more bears on baits than the average person, and know my shooting ability with a rifle or muzzle-loader, I generally place my stands thirty yards or so from the bait.

Base your own shooting distance on your comfort level, shooting ability, and the type of weapon used. The farther away the better, but fifty yards is around the maximum when using rifles and muzzleloaders. For bows and handguns, it's more like twenty or thirty yards. A bear's heart and lung area is lower than some other game animals, and shooting from a high, close stand may set a trajectory that's too steep.

Since many guides and outfitters use the same bait sites year after year, they long ago built permanent stands made of two-by-fours and plywood, with wooden ladders leading up to them. In many states and provinces, these stands are no longer allowed. Before establishing a bait site, hunters should be familiar with any local laws pertaining to stands.

Today, portable treestands and ladder stands are the norm. Portables are light enough to be carried into bait sites and can be set at any desired height. They require some kind of foot pegs or steps to set up and access; screw-in types are quite popular. The screw-in types aren't legal everywhere because they scar trees, but a climbing stick (a straight piece of steel with offset rungs for easy climbing) or strap-on steps can be used instead. They work just as well and don't damage trees.

Ladder stands are also popular, and I actually prefer them to most portables. They are bulkier, which makes them harder to get into some bait sites, but once set in place they can be left for the season. Some good ones are available for less than a hundred dollars. They don't damage trees, and can be made quite comfortable compared to most bargain portables. Ladder stands vary in height from around twelve to sixteen feet, which is plenty high. Extensions are generally available if needed.

The so-called climbing portable stand can be used, too, but it requires a fairly straight tree without large limbs. Also, the stand should be carried in and out each time it's used.

The average shot over bait is less than thirty yards.

I usually avoid ground blinds. My experience has been that they increase the chances of being discovered because your scent is at ground level, and although bears most often use regular trails to enter a bait area, you can't always count on it. Where adequate trees aren't present, ground stands may be the only viable option. They should be located a bit farther back from the bait and completely conceal the hunter from all directions, if possible.

One of the biggest problems for hunters sitting over bait is remaining still for long periods of time. Bears are forgiving of movement in some situations, but most will spook when startled. Several years ago I started reading paperback novels on stand. I also do crossword puzzles. In fact, I do most of my reading these days on stand. Not only does it pass the time, but it also helps me keep quiet. Before turning each page I slowly look up to see what is going on, first with my eyes and then by turning my head. I've become a master at turning the page without making a sound. And even when engrossed in a good read, I can stay tuned in to any sounds in the forest.

No matter how comfortable a stand is, you'll eventually need to move, to make slight adjustments and stretch muscles. Do so slowly, as quietly and briefly as possible, and only after making sure no animals are visible. Continue to keep a sharp eye out dur-

Ground blinds should be well concealed and take advantage of prevailing winds. Most hunters use them only if hanging stands isn't possible.

ing the process. To minimize movements on stand, have a place handy where you can rest or hang your weapon for quick use. The same goes for any backpacks and fanny-packs.

Many stand hunters take a shot before the timing is right. People get nervous and excited when they see a bear, and all too often they snap off a poorly placed shot. Take your time. Suck in and slowly release a few deep breaths. Relax. Get your heart back in your chest and regulate your breathing. I've always found it best to sit still, following the bear with your eyes and slow adjustments of the head until it actually starts to feed. Then, and only then, should you pick up your rifle or bow and prepare to shoot. Never take your eyes off that animal. If it stops feeding and lifts its head to look around, freeze. Wait until it resumes eating to finish getting into position. Once the bear is again fully occupied, a slight noise will probably only cause it to lift its head before going back to the bait.

Bears are always curious. On occasion, they have walked beneath my stand, around it, put their front legs on the lower rungs of the ladder, looked right up at me, and taken a sniff. They are only checking things out. Sit back and remain still, keeping your eyes on the bear. In nearly thirty years of hunting black bears I have never had one actually try to climb into a

Sitting quietly for long periods is important when hunting over bait. Novels and cross-word puzzles help pass the time.

stand. If you feel threatened, make a noise and the bear will probably bolt out of there.

HUNTING WITH HOUNDS

Hunting black bears and trailing wounded bears with hounds is legal in seventeen states and four provinces. Like hunting over bait, the practice is a favorite target for anti-hunt and animal rights groups. Whether the use of hounds is ethical or sporting is subjective, but for me it's a fun, thrilling way to kill a bear.

But it's also much more than that. For folks who own hounds—and for many who don't but participate whenever possible—the kill is secondary. It's the chase, seeing and hearing the hounds work, the excitement of it all. Owning and running hounds is a way of life, not just a type of hunting. Raising, breeding, and hunting with dogs is something that takes a long-term commitment and a lot of free time.

It means working them as often as possible, not just during hunting season. Many states have special seasons just for training, when bears may be pursued but not killed. There are also trial events during the off-season to help keep the hounds sharp.

Owning a pack of hounds takes a considerable amount of money. Hounds from good bloodlines require an investment of several hundred to several thousand dollars. A good strike dog generally costs more. By the time training is complete and the necessary equipment purchased, the dollars really add up. And most houndmen don't own just one dog; usually they have at least two or three, perhaps a half dozen or more. Large packs can make hunting a confusing affair. Splitting the dogs up into two or three teams also gives them a break between hunts.

Hunting with hounds has a long history in this country. George Washington was an enthusiastic houndman, as were many early settlers. In those days, much of the hunting was for raccoons, foxes, and other smaller animals. But the most popular breeds were equally adept at chasing bear, and today those dogs are specifically trained for this purpose.

In the old days, hounds were so popular because they offered the only practical method of hunting. The middle and southern Appalachians are extremely rugged hill country, covered with thick laurel, brambles, and other

Hunting with hounds can be physically challenging.

brush that made it virtually impossible to hunt bears any other way. The best bear country still looks like this today, and since baiting is generally prohibited in this region, hounds remain popular. In areas where baiting and hounds are both legal, many outfitters use dogs primarily to track wounded bears.

A good bear hound must possess certain characteristics. In general, hounds should weigh forty to sixty-five pounds so that they can run long distances at high speeds and remain agile enough to keep a bear occupied while dodging out of harm's way in close quarters. Although there are exceptions, larger dogs are usually slower, which increases their chances of getting hurt or even killed. Good hounds often look thin, even underfed, but a closer examination will show that they are actually well conditioned and muscled.

A good bear dog must also be bright, confident, and courageous enough to keep game at bay on the ground or when treed. It should possess solid treeing instincts, good endurance for all-day runs, a loud, steady mouth that enables the hunter to locate it, take readily to water, and possess a good nose that can detect and follow fresh or old sign.

Good bear hounds allow you to hunt very rugged country.

Hounds with these abilities are no ordinary dogs, and good ones are hard to find, which is one reason hound hunts are almost always more expensive than bait hunts. Bait hunts with guides and outfitters normally vary from $500 to $1,800, depending on the location and services rendered, but hound hunts generally start at around $2,000 and go up from there.

Due to the long history of hound hunting in North America, the fraternity of houndmen has developed its own vocabulary over the years. The first time I hunted bears with hounds, I recall the head guide instructing one of his assistants to "take that Walker bitch and put her in the strike box, will ya? She's had a good cold nose lately. Let's see if she's still got it." I had no idea what he was talking about, as my definition of "bitch" evidently differed from his, and I couldn't see why a cold nose would be better than a hot one. I had a lot to learn!

Over the years, I got to know what "breaking scent," "cold nose," "hot nose," "loose mouth," "backtrack," and a host of other terms meant. Anyone planning to hunt with hounds should have at least a basic knowledge of this unique language. The following list should get you started.

HOUND-HUNTING LINGO

Backtrack: Used when a hound is running a track in the opposite direction from the one the game animal is traveling.

Barks Per Minute: Number of barks during each minute while trailing or treeing.

Bawl Mouth: Long, drawn-out barks.

Baying: The bark a hound makes when it locates a game animal on the ground.

Bitch: A female dog.

Blanketback: A hound with a back that is black or nearly so, resembling a blanket.

Bloodline: A hound's pedigree.

Box Dog (Rig or Strike Dog): A hound that rides on top of the dog box in the back of the truck or in the strike cage to detect, or "strike," game.

Breaking Scent: The scent of unwanted game, which is used to break a hound from running that particular animal.

Brood Bitch: A female hound used primarily for producing pups.

Broke Dog: A hound trained not to chase unwanted game.

Cat Foot: A hound that is short-toed and round-footed, with knuckles high and well developed like a cat's.

Changeover Bark: A noticeable change in a hound's bark that indicates it's no longer trailing a game animal, but now has it treed.

Check In: A hound that will range out looking for a track then come back, or "check in," when none is found.

Check Dog: A "broke" hound that will come back to the hunter if the other dogs are chasing "off game." Used primarily to help train pups.

Close Hunter: A hound that stays close while looking for a scent trail.

Cold Nose: Denotes a hound that can smell an old track (cold trail) that has little scent.

Dam: A female hound that has birthed pups.

Dew Claws: The false toe and claw on a dog's foreleg.

Finished Hound: A hound that is fully trained to only run desired game.

Freeze Brand: A permanent mark with letters, numbers, or a design applied to the hound for identification. A patch of dog hair is shaved off and then a brand dipped in alcohol or dry ice (to lower the temperature) is pressed into the skin. It works by changing the hair color in the shaved area to white.

Full Cry: A hound's bark that means it's on a hot trail or scent.

Gyp: A young bitch that hasn't been bred.

Hot Nose: A hound that will only work a fresh track.

Ill Dog: A hound that likes to fight with other hounds.

Junk Game: Undesired game animals.

Loose Mouth: A hound that bays or barks for no reason (without smelling game or scent).

Off-Game: Used to describe a hound that is running unwanted game.

Open: A hound's bark that announces when a track has been located.

Pressure Tree Dog: A hound that keeps game treed until the hunter arrives, refusing to leave for any reason.

Pup Trainer: An experienced hound that is hunted with a pup.

Scent Drag: A piece of cloth coated with scent or an animal skin dragged along the ground to help train hounds.

Silent (Running Silent): When a hound runs a track or trail without barking.

Sire: A hound that has fathered pups.

Slick (Dead) Tree: When the hound and/or hunter arrives at the tree but the game animal isn't there.

Strike: When a hound detects scent and starts to bark.

Tight Mouth: A hound that does not open up much (bark) on track or trail.

Track Drifter: A hound that works a track or trail by taking shortcuts away from the direct trail.

Track Straddler: A hound that follows a track by smelling every step a game animal has made.

Tracking (Telemetry) Collar: A dog collar with a transmitter that emits a signal that can be tracked with a receiver. It's used to locate lost dogs after the hunt, as well as dogs on tree.

Treed Bark: The bark used when a hound is at the tree where the game animal has taken refuge.

Wide Hunter: A hound that hunts a long distance away from the hunter.

CHOOSING A BREED

Although in times past many types of dog were used to run game, just five breeds are specially trained for hunting bears these days. Each breed possesses the basic characteristics necessary, but there's endless debate about which is the best. The truth is, each breed has its good dogs and not-so-good dogs, and not all dogs of a particular breed are worth owning.

One of the most popular breeds is the Plott. Of the five top breeds, it's the only one that doesn't trace its ancestry to the fox-hound. Bred specifically for stamina and gameness, the ancestors of today's Plott were primarily used for boar hunting in Germany. When they first landed on American shores around 1750, wild boars were not available, but they performed very well hunting 'coon and bears in the western mountains of North Carolina. The Plott breed has been registered with the United Kennel Club (UKC) since 1946, and these dogs are famous for their courage and endurance. They have clear voices that carry well and are active, fast, bright, and confident. Plotts are also vigorous fighters on game, possess excellent treeing instinct, take well to water, and are quick to learn.

Plotts, Walkers, and bluetick hounds are among the most popular breeds.

The Walker is another popular dog for bear hunting. The breed was developed from certain strains of English Walker foxhounds, and its ancestors first arrived in Albemarle County, Virginia, around 1742, and later in Kentucky. These dogs became the foundation for the so-called "Virginia" hounds, which were developed into the present-day Walker. They have been registered with the UKC since 1945, first as Walkers, and then as Treeing Walkers. They are energetic and intelligent, highly active, composed, and confident, with lots of endurance and trailing, hunting, and treeing ability.

The bluetick also is descended from the English foxhounds, with some blood from various French hounds that were used for big game hunting. It's a beautiful dog, generally known for its dark-blue, thickly mottled coat with black spots on the back, ears, and side. It was first registered with the UKC in 1946. The bluetick is an active and ambitious runner known for its speed on the trail.

The black and tan is another breed that can trace its ancestry from the American foxhound and Virginia foxhounds of colonial times. Some bloodhound stock is also included, which probably explains its coloration, tendency to be larger-boned than other breeds, long ears, and famous cold nose. Going further back, the black and tan can be traced to the English foxhounds, and before that to the Tolbot and St. Hubert hounds of France. These hounds were first brought to England following the Norman invasions in the eleventh century. The American black and tan was the first coonhound breed to be registered with the UKC (in 1900). They are known to be active, fast, bright, confident, and courageous, with excellent trailing and treeing instincts.

The foundation for the modern redbone hound came from George F. L. Birdsong, a noted fox hunter and hound breeder

Foxhounds and coonhounds make great bear dogs.

from Georgia. In the 1840s Birdsong obtained a pack of reddish coonhounds, which he crossed with a pack of bloodhounds. Although the overall coloration of the offspring was red, these first dogs were called "saddle bags" due to a black saddlelike marking on the back. The saddle was bred out and the solid red dogs became known as redbone coonhounds. In 1902 the redbone became the second coonhound breed to be registered with the UKC. It's medium-built, striking in color, agile, and highly proficient on the trail and at treeing game.

THE CHASE

There are several ways to hunt bears with hounds. One of the most common is by employing a strike, or rig, dog. The rig dog is often placed in the back of a pickup on a short leash to prevent it from jumping out, sometimes on top of a box holding the other dogs. But many guides, outfitters, and hunters who use hounds a great deal have a box or cage mounted on the front of their vehicles specifically for this purpose.

Once the rig dog is in position, the guide will drive a network of back roads in areas where bears are known to frequent until the dog picks up, or strikes, scent. This is a good method in areas with a network of old logging roads because it's possible to cover a lot of ground. Bears often have to cross these roads as they roam about. The road network also makes it easier to get close to and/or retrieve the game animal and the hounds after the run.

In other situations, hounds are led to areas where bears have been actively feeding. Fields of corn or grain, apple orchards, and other agricultural areas are hot places to start. The devastation left behind by feeding bears is often easy to spot, as are trails leading to and from these places. Farmers are usually more than happy to be rid of a problem bear. Natural food areas and bait sites are also good places to start a hound hunt.

The rig dog is typically the one used to find scent worth pursuing, so these hounds have to be something special. Usually, this dog is the most experienced and best trained of the bunch, but in a few rare cases it's a younger dog with great natural ability. A rig dog is a born hunter and leader. The best ones hunt all day, are smart enough to sound off only on bears, strike a track in the right direction, and have well-balanced mouths, which just means they're vocal enough to get the other dogs involved quickly and keep them involved without over-barking. A dog that opens its mouth too much on a track often confuses the pack, causing it to travel away from game. On the other hand, a dog that doesn't bark enough on track often gets to the bear alone. To say the least, a good rig dog is a very valuable asset.

Once the rig dog strikes a track, anything can happen. Experienced guides can often figure things out and plan accordingly—which way the track is going and where to head off the chase to bring it to a quick and successful end—but nothing is guaranteed. In areas where roads are available, bears are sometimes shot crossing ahead of the dogs before they can be treed because the guide was able to determine where a bear was traveling and cut it off. But more times than not, once a bear knows it's being pursued and dogs are hot on the trail the hunt becomes an all-day event. This is particularly true of older boars that have managed to survive by using their wits.

In most cases, bears take to the thickest cover available, travel over endless hills, and do whatever else they can to elude the dogs. The search for fresh sign usually starts early in the morning in order to get as much out of the day as possible. Some guides I've hunted with refuse to let loose the dogs after a certain hour because they fear losing the daylight. Others avoid certain conditions. For example, wind makes it difficult to hear dogs ranging far out, and rain often washes away a scent trail.

A hound hunt usually covers a lot of ground. The older I get, the more I become convinced that this is a game for the young of body and heart. It's a good idea to do some extra walking, hiking, and running for a few weeks before participating in this type of hunt. Even guides, outfitters, and hunters who use hounds on a regular basis get worn out at times. Experienced houndmen learn to listen to the dogs carefully and anticipate the bear's next move before running wildly ahead.

Professional guides often equip their hounds, or at least the strike dog, with tracking collars. These collars can be invaluable for getting a fix on the direction of the chase or for locating treeing hounds or lost hounds. Many times, dogs that lose a track drift back to where the hunt started or to the nearest road—but not always—and tracking collars save a lot of time. They are especially helpful if a dog is injured or killed.

Carrying CB radios (or walkie-talkies) is also a good idea. Hunting bears with hounds is usually a team effort, and if hunters become separated CBs allow them to stay in communication.

Electronic tracking equipment is often necessary to locate a hound.

They allow hunters to discuss where the chase is going, where to meet or cut off a bear, and how to lay out the best line of approach to a treed bear. If a hunter is injured or lost, CBs can literally be a lifesaver, as well. Along with CBs, a compass or GPS and a map of the area are helpful. I also carry a small fannypack and backpack with a flashlight, water, emergency food, snacks, matches, first-aid kit, rain gear, safety blankets, dry socks, and extra ammo.

Clothing can be important, too. If hunting with a guide, ask whether you will be a runner (someone actually in pursuit much of the time), or whether you'll be standing at a crossing. On many hunts, you'll be some of each. I like to dress comfortably in layers, which can be peeled off to prevent overheating. Simply add them back on if you're placed on a crossing for long periods, or after the hunt.

Boots that fit properly, are light, and keep the feet dry and warm are critical. Some hunters like boots with leather or hard-rubber bottoms with canvas tops with holes in the sides. These boots are generally light, offer good ankle and arch support, and allow water to drain, which is important when crossing brooks, rivers, and swamps. My standard footwear is the Maine Hunting Shoe by L.L. Bean.

A spring black bear taken with hounds in Idaho.

The best outcome from a chase is a treed bear, as this is usually the safest scenario for hunters and dogs, but the bear isn't always accommodating. In some cases, bears refuse to tree, and after making a brief stand they'll depart to continue the run. Some bears never tree, particularly large boars and sows traveling alone, which often make long treks ahead of the dogs, stopping periodically to rest. In such cases, two groups of hunters, one following the dogs and the other coming in from the opposite direction, may be necessary to force the bear off the ground or into making a stand.

Moving in on a treed bear or a bear at bay is an exciting, adrenalin-pumping experience. It is also something to take seriously, particularly when a bear is on the ground. It will often take refuge in thick cover, where visibility is restricted, or position itself facing its attackers with ears back, hackles raised, and teeth clattering. The bear may be moving around to hold off the dogs, even false charging, so a slow, carefully planned advance is a must. Stay downwind and out of sight as much as possible when a bear is at bay on the ground, since bears that see humans will often make a mad dash.

I have had bears run right at me, avoiding harm only because I was able to slip behind a tree. These bears were probably more concerned with fleeing the scene than hurting me, but it's an experience not soon forgotten. If the bear breaks free again the hounds are quick to take pursuit, and the run is usually, but not always, short. The trick is to get close enough, ideally without begin detected, for a quick kill. This usually means a head shot, which isn't easy because the dogs are probably circling and lunging to keep the bear occupied. You never want to take a shot that may injure a dog, but you also don't want to deal with a wounded bear.

Bears that have treed can usually be dealt with more safely. In most situations, the dogs are pulled back and tied off, allowing the bear and the hunters to relax a little. The hunters now have time to decide the best way to handle things. First, take note of how the bear is situated. It will often be sitting or lying on a limb, hiding a clear shot to the vitals. But each situation is different. The head shot usually affords the quickest kill, but that may not be an option if it's a trophy skull. If circumstances don't allow a clean kill, it's best to let the bear go, or at least have everyone back off until the bear leaves the tree, at which point the chase can continue.

If the bear is in a shootable position, the head guide will instruct everyone on how to handle the situation. The primary shooter should be supported by backup shooters in case the bear is not dead when it hits the ground, and every shooter should know where and when to safely shoot. Sometimes the bear will hang in the tree a while until it feels safe enough to move, at other times it will retreat quickly and hit the ground running, providing no time to shoot. One thing is certain, though. The first shot is critical and should kill the bear in the tree. A wounded bear that falls to the ground is extremely dangerous to dogs and hunters.

OTHER HUNTING TACTICS

If bait and hounds aren't legal where you want to hunt, other methods can still be effective. These tactics include spot-and-stalk, still-hunting, coordinated drives, tracking in snow, predator calling, or, when water is scarce, hunting near reliable water sources. A combination of these tactics is often used, but nearly all of them revolve around hunting the bruin in areas where natural or agricultural foods are readily available. Recognizing foods that bears like, and knowing where to find them, becomes even more important for hunter success.

In many areas, spot-and-stalk is a productive method, although it usually requires a great deal of time and patience. But the stalk is always exciting, and quite a challenge. The hunter often starts by taking a high position overlooking a feeding area where bears have been seen previously or where sign has been detected. He then methodically glasses the area at long distance.

Some hunters prefer spotting scopes, others binoculars. Spotting scopes are generally more powerful, so they can be more useful for determining sex, overall size, color phase, pelt condition, and potential head size, as well as possible trails leading to feeding areas. They are attached to a tripod, which enables the hunter to hold on intended targets for long periods. But spotting scopes can be cumbersome to lug around, particularly when hiking long distances or when using horses, as is sometimes the case in remote regions of the West and far North. They can also be hard on the eyes after prolonged use. Some of the most popular brands include Nikon, Swarvoski, Leupold, Simmons, Tasco, and Burris. The 60X is a good choice for long-range spotting.

High-magnification binoculars work well, too. They should be at least 8x50 power; 10x50 and 12x50 are even better because they're more powerful and let in more light. Binocular are easier to carry around in the field, but they can be difficult to hold steady for long periods, and the image has a tendency to bounce around. Many manufacturers that offer spotting scopes also make binoculars, and Bushnell, Kahles, Zeiss, Leica, Steiner, and Pentax all make quality binoculars.

The new stabilizing binoculars are great. They look like binoculars and are easy to tote afield, but they offer an internal gyroscope system that greatly reduces the image shake so common in high-magnification binoculars. The image is also razorsharp. The Image Stabilizer Binocular from Canon and Nikon's Stabileyes VR Binocular are two of the very best. The higher-power models are more expensive than regular high-magnification glasses of comparable power, even some of the better spotting scopes, but for the serious hunter planning to spot-and-stalk game they are well worth the investment.

Once a bear is spotted, the fun begins. Taking prevailing wind into consideration, you must pick out the best line of approach using whatever cover and terrain is available. This is the real challenge. As noted earlier, the black bear has a keen sense of smell, so it's imperative to stay downwind during the stalk. It is also necessary to watch for changing wind currents. Be as quiet as possible and try to keep the bear in sight, although that is not always possible. It helps to take note of landmarks—a certain tree or group of trees, a rock outcropping—that can be used as directional markers when the bear isn't visible.

I like to use as much natural cover as possible during the stalk, especially ravines and gullies that help funnel scent away and muffle sound. They also allow the hunter to move faster. The same is true of moving water. But remember that a feeding bear will often move, so emerge from cover cautiously and scan the area well. I once made what I thought was a perfect stalk on a bear, but when I arrived where I thought he would be he had moved a hundred yards to my right, up a hill. He spotted me first and was gone.

It is important to hunt with your eyes, never take anything for granted, and expect any possibility. Your ears will also tell you a lot. Bears can be noisy feeders, and on quiet days it's often possible to hear them eating fifty yards away, particularly when they're heavily into wild cherries and other fruit patches.

Since I hunt with a muzzleloader much of the time, I usually need to get as close as possible—under a hundred yards, closer if possible. But don't press beyond what the wind and cover will allow. Know your limitations with gun or bow, and pass on shots you can't be sure of. There is always another day, and the bear may very well return to the same area if he isn't spooked.

Combining stalking with still-hunting is another productive tactic, particularly when bears are known to be feeding heavily on natural foods in woodland areas and along waterways. Working into the wind, moving slow without sound, and hunting with your eyes and ears will bring you the most success. When bears are engrossed with stuffing their bellies, particularly in spring and fall, it may be possible to get extremely close, even within bow or pistol range.

At other times, still-hunting along natural travel corridors such as hillsides, slopes, spurs, creek beds, and open ridges can be productive. You may be able to intercept a bear traveling from a bedding area to a food source, or one moving between food sources. Early morning and late afternoon are often the best times for this type of hunt, but when bears are active they can be seen at any time of day.

Across much of Canada, the upper Midwest, and the Northeast, it's possible to use canoes to hunt bears. These regions are blessed with a lot of waterways, which are often remote. Wild cherries, brambles, and other desirable foods often grow close to water, and a canoe offers a quiet way to access these potential hotspots. Upon reaching such an area, still-hunting tactics are usually employed. Where plenty of fresh sign is discovered, sitting in a makeshift or natural blind overlooking these feeding stations can be rewarding. In arid regions like the Southwest, using water to locate bears is also productive.

Sitting, still-hunting, or slowly stalking the edges of cornfields and orchards in bear country is another good technique, particularly just before dark and at dawn, when bears are most likely to visit these areas. One productive tactic is to locate primary trails leading into these areas, and then take up a position at a high observation point, perhaps one or two hundred yards inside the wood line. Bears often move in close but hang back until the cover of darkness, and if your timing is right you can catch them within shooting hours.

In northern areas where early snow is possible, hunters can often track bears on fresh snow before they den up for the winter.

Where only spot-and-stalk hunting is allowed, good binoculars come in handy.

Bears tracked later in the season are usually boars, because sows, especially sows with cubs, generally den up earlier. In Maine, where I live, the bear season stretches into the November deer season, and on several occasions I've run across fresh bear sign in the snow while looking for whitetails. I can never resist following fresh bear tracks, and twice I've been rewarded for my efforts.

On one occasion I was lucky enough to catch a small male rummaging for nuts in a beechnut tree north of Moosehead Lake. There were three or four inches of fresh snow on the ground, just enough to make it possible to walk without any noise, and I almost walked right past him. When I got to the tree the tracks mysteriously disappeared, and I actually stood there wondering where the hell he went. After a minute or so I heard a limb snap overhead. When I looked up he was staring down at me. The bear had been so occupied he hadn't even heard me approach; he seemed as surprised as I was. I had tracked the bear for less than two hours and shot him under a half-mile from my truck.

My second opportunity wasn't quite so easy. It was the first week of November, and I cut a fresh track just three hundred yards behind my home. They appeared to have been made that morning, so just in case, I returned to the house and loaded up a small backpack with snacks, water, a flashlight and extra batteries, matches, a compass, a walkie-talkie and some other supplies. I told my wife what was going on and then headed out. The last thing she said to me was, "See you tonight, or whenever." Little did we know . . .

I followed those tracks all day, managing to kill the bear just before dark in another town about five miles away. By the time I hiked out of the woods to call my wife from a gas station, it was around eight o'clock, more than twelve hours since I left the house and well after dark. The next day was Sunday, a no-hunting day in Maine, so when I got home I called the game warden and told him what had happened. After getting permission, my brother, a couple of friends, and I went to retrieve the bear the next day.

I learned a lot about tracking bears that day. Anyone trailing a bear in snow should pack some survival essentials and be physically fit. By the time I shot the bear I was exhausted, and I'd been thinking about heading for the nearest road to call it a day.

Bears use a lot of tricks when they know they're being followed. At times that day I saw where the bear had actually backtracked, and at one point it had climbed a steep ridge so it could look back in my direction. It even crossed a log over a stream, which cost me some time because the log was so small I had to move upstream to find another way over. Other hunters have told me they've had bears make wide loops, circling around to get a glimpse at what is on their trail or to pick up scent. Some make an all-day jaunt out of looping back nearly to where the game started. They may even loop around and start following the hunter.

One hunter told me he once observed a spot where a bear had jumped from rock to rock then to a place bare of snow, leaving no tracks. He only figured it out after carefully circling the area, which allowed him to pick up the tracks on the other side of the rocks.

Tracking is fun and challenging, but it's important to be prepared for anything. Work with the wind and move swiftly but silently. Under the right conditions, tracking is a supreme test of hunting skills and woodsmanship.

Predator calls also work on bears, but it's important to call in an area where scouting has revealed strong sign and/or good food sources. I like to combine calling with spotting tactics, working a bear only after I've seen it. This always beats calling cold in areas where no bears have been seen or spotted.

It's important to have some cover and a commanding view from above of the possible approach area, at least 220 degrees. And don't neglect to consider wind direction. Ideally, the wind should be nonexistent or blowing across your position, which means hitting your ear or cheek when you're facing the most likely approach direction. On several stalks, after getting as close as I could with the limited cover, I've been able to draw bears in farther by calling.

Calling in heavy winds is usually a waste of time, simply because it's hard to call loudly enough for a bear to hear you at a distance. And any bear in the area is more likely to pick up your scent. Choose your terrain carefully. In deep basins, creek and river bottoms, and heavy timber it may take more time for bears to respond because sound doesn't carry as well; the opposite is often true in desert habitat and on open hardwood ridges. In most cases, it's best to start calling only after you spot a bear and move into a position close enough for it to hear you.

If you're cold calling, start by calling loudly and often, even aggressively, for thirty to sixty minutes, and then taper off to intermittent calls. A bear will quickly lose interest if you stop calling too soon, but it's important to always be on the lookout. Once you see a bear, call only enough to keep it interested. Again, natural feeding areas and around bait sites are good places to start, since bears often rest around their food supplies. If nothing happens after an hour or so, move to another spot and start over.

The most popular calls imitate injured rabbits and small rodents, like mice. Handheld or electronic devices can be used, but check their legality in your hunting area. I prefer electronic calls because most models can be placed at a distance but controlled from your sitting position, either by remote control or with a long extension cord. This allows the hunter to place the speaker in a position so the bear won't approach directly toward him, often providing a better shot opportunity. Tapes are programmed at the right pitch and intervals or duration, and some even come with ground-movement sounds such as thrashing leaves and hops.

Rabbit and mouse calls seem to work anytime, but my greatest success with them has come in the spring, before soft and hard mast becomes available. Fawn bleats have been known to work, too, especially in the spring when fawns are most vulnerable, although I've had little personal experience with them.

Calling with a partner is usually safer and more productive. The hunters can face in opposite directions, covering all possible approaches with a minimum of movement.

In some states, organized drives can be a productive way to hunt bears. The tactic is popular in Pennsylvania, where groups will get together to work a particular swamp, patch of woods, or hardwood ridge much as they would deer. Drivers try to push bears toward places where they have to cross open ground, and shooters are posted nearby.

Some big bears are taken this way, but most tend to be smaller or younger because these bears are more likely to panic and run. The big boys are apt to stay put or circle around the drive. Driving is only legal in few jurisdictions, so check the regulations where you intend to hunt.

Chapter

4

RIFLES AND CARTRIDGES

One of the biggest dilemmas facing the first-time bear hunter is selecting a firearm, caliber, and load. Too many hunters simply don't understand this critter. Black bears are often pursued with the same large-caliber rifles and heavy loads used for brown or grizzly bears. But comparing black bears to their larger cousins is like comparing apples to oranges, or maybe apples to watermelons. The black bear is by far the smallest of the group, and though some of the big-bore rifles and magnum calibers have a place in certain situations, such firepower really isn't necessary to quickly and humanely dispatch the average bruin.

Frankly, there are so many calibers and loads available that it's difficult to make sense of them all. I've been writing about hunting and guns for over three decades, but I'll be the first to admit I don't understand it all. One expert might suggest that a .30–06 loaded with 150-grain factory loads is the best choice for black bears. Another might say a .300 Winchester Magnum pushing a 180-grain Nosler Partition, while someone else might recommend something completely different.

All opinions are subjective, of course. And the recommendations of some "pros" are all too often based on what pro-team they

Which rifle and caliber you choose for black bears will depend on a variety of factors, but for most situations, your deer rifle will probably work just fine.

happen to be on. I've shot a lot of black bears over the years, more than the average guy, and in a wider variety of habitats and situations, and I'll stick my neck out here and say that black bears can usually be taken cleanly with standard deer calibers and loads. However, large bears and specific hunting conditions may dictate that you go a little heavier at times.

But worrying about the best rifle caliber and load is putting the cart before the horse. It's the responsibility of every ethical hunter to kill game as quickly and humanely as possible, and this requires more than just firepower. Shot placement is a factor, too. No matter how fast or powerful a load is, it still has to hit the animal where it counts.

No matter what weapon or caliber you choose, you must practice enough to know your capabilities before heading afield.

Nearly all my black bear and big game hunting is done with muzzleloaders, and to be quite honest, I have trouble with accuracy over 150 yards, even with scopes and the new "magnum" front-loaders. So I never take a shot at that range.

Any firearm should be properly sighted in before a hunt. This is best done at a range, off a benchrest and using the same loads you plan to hunt with. Different bullets often have different points of impact, and even bullets of the same weight or caliber made by different manufacturers may vary in performance. It helps to pick a cartridge, and maker, and stick with it. The same is true for muzzleloaders. Once you hit on the proper powder charge and projectile combination, stay the course.

It is just as important to make sure the firearm is still sighted in once you arrive at camp, particularly if you're flying to your hunting destination, but also if you're banging down rough dirt

Spend some time at the range testing various loads and sighting in, and you'll have a better chance of bringing home a bear.

roads. It never ceases to amaze me that no matter how much care is taken in packing a rifle, its accuracy can be compromised in travel. It only takes a few minutes to check things out upon arrival and before hunting, and you may be glad you did. There are so many things you can't control on a hunt that it makes no sense at all to shoot with a gun not properly sighted in or without knowing its effective killing range and accuracy with specific loads—all things you can do easily with a little forethought.

Practice is the key; get in as much as possible. For example, if you're planning a bait hunt from elevated stands, particularly if hunting with an outfitter or guide, find out the shooting range and height of the stands and practice accordingly. Practice shooting from different positions because not all stands set up by guides and outfitters will offer the best seating arrangements. While in the stand, practice moving without making noise.

It's not uncommon for a hunter to hang his rifle or bow or to rest it across the knees while waiting for a bear to come into a bait site. Practice reaching for it or lifting it and getting into shooting position, again without sound. Do this slowly, keeping your eyes on the target at all times, just as you should when actually hunting.

Conventional firearm, handgun, and in-line muzzleloader hunters should practice flipping the safety into firing position, again keeping an eye on the target and without any sound. Side-lock muzzleloader enthusiasts should be able to pull back the hammer with a minimum of noise, and bowhunters should practice nocking their arrows with little or no head movement.

It's also important to practice breathing. Yes, breathing. I know from experience with bruins and other big game that it's next to impossible to shoot accurately while you're breathing heavily. Even today, after so many years in bear country, when a monster boar or color-phase bear comes into view, my heart starts to pound, my breaths come in short bursts, and I feel like I've just run a hundred-yard dash. In the last chapter, I mentioned how important it is to remain still until the bear actually gets on the bait, because once it starts to eat it relaxes and its attention is focused elsewhere. But it also provides time for the hunter to get himself under control. This is just as true when making a stalk or hunting with hounds; take a few minutes to settle down and get your breathing as normal as possible before you shoot.

This is easy to do. Simply take in a deep breath, hold it, and let it out slowly. You should immediately feel yourself relax, but repeat this as many times as necessary until you're ready. You may never fully relax due to the excitement, but you can't get off a good shot while actually breathing, so once you're ready to shoot, take in a final deep breath, let it partway out, and pull the trigger, finishing the exhale after taking the shot. Practice this technique on the range while sighting in and while simulating different hunting scenarios and you will undoubtedly improve your accuracy. Pretty soon, it'll just be automatic, you won't even have to think about it.

If you're planning a spot-and-stalk hunt with a rifle, practice at ranges out to two hundred yards or so. Or if you'll be hunting with a professional, ask your guide or outfitter what the expected shooting distance will be. Just as important, practice shooting across a ravine or small gully and downward from a hillside at various ranges. Make yourself proficient while kneeling, sitting, prone—any position you can think of—and with a variety of impromptu rests (boulders, trees, etc.).

In addition to lots of practice time, make sure your trigger pull is set properly. Most of us purchase a rifle and go to work with the trigger weight set at the factory. We get used to it over time, but it's often set too heavy for really accurate shooting. Due to liability concerns, most manufacturers set triggers at five or six pounds, but you can have an experienced gunsmith adjust the

This Idaho boar was taken with a .308 loaded with a 180-grain bullet, which is more than suitable out to 200 yards.

trigger pull to two and a half to three pounds. A lighter trigger pull is easier to control, requires less pressure, and reduces the changes of "pulling" the shot, yet still provides sufficient room to call off the shot if necessary. At one time, fully adjustable triggers were quite common, but today, either because of lawsuits or the design of firing mechanisms, most lever-actions, semi-automatics, and pumps are not. The same is true of most muzzleloaders. Many bolt-actions, however, are adjustable, and a lighter pull will prove advantageous.

You'll also need a suitable sight system, which normally means a scope these days. Scopes magnify the target, making it easier to see the animal and pick the proper aiming point. They also provide a single sight plane. Unlike open sights, where the eye continuously tries to focus from rear to front sight to target, scopes make it possible to focus solely on the target. Lastly, scopes are better in low-light conditions, such as early and late in the day when the sun is at a low angle or in shadowed areas. A quality scope that gathers light can extend prime hunting time by several minutes each day, which is important when hunting black bears.

Scope magnification is vital, too. When hunting black bears over bait, scope power isn't a big factor because most shots are made at well under seventy-five yards. But with a spot-and-stalk

This New Brunswick bear was taken with a scoped .30-06. Scopes offer an advantage in low-light conditions and allow the hunter to make the best shot placement.

shot at two hundred yards magnification makes all the difference. Because most of us hunt a variety of big game, at short and long distances, with only one or two favorite firearms, variable scopes are a good way to go. The 3–9X variable scope is probably the most popular one on the market these days, but for most bear hunting 9X magnification is overkill. Even at two hundred yards, 6X is usually more than enough.

Setting a scope too high can actually cost you game, because as the magnification increases the field of view decreases, and it gets harder to hold on the target. For all the bears I've taken with high-powered centerfire rifles out to two hundred yards magnification between 3X and 5X proved sufficient. Over bait or with hounds, 1½X to 2X was more than enough. My recommendation for a good variable scope for centerfire rifles, muzzleloaders, and slug guns ranges from 1½X to 5X, with a good second choice being

2½X to 8X. Just remember to set it at 1½X to 3X if hunting over bait or hounds, and between 3X and 5X when spot-and-stalk hunting.

Fixed scopes are a viable option, too. They are less expensive, less complicated, and slightly lighter. One set at 2X to 3X should provide all the magnification necessary at close range or out to nearly two hundred yards.

When it comes to reticles, crosshairs, post, dot, or some combination of each, it's really a matter of personal preference. I like the plex-type crosshair, where the hairs are thick toward the outside but taper in the middle where they cross. I think the eye finds, and flows to, the cross faster and more naturally, particularly in low light. Scopes with dots, and even those with crosshairs, can cause you problems in low-light conditions, as can standard crosshairs, although I prefer them to a straight post with crosshair.

With any scope, make sure it's correctly and securely mounted, and be sure it provides a full field of view when the rifle hits your shoulder. It should also offer plenty of eye relief. The last thing you want to deal with while aiming at a bear is shifting your head or moving the rifle forward or back to get things lined up. When you raise that rifle, the scope should be right on.

See-through mounts are common on big game guns, and they work reasonably well on bears at relative close range, such as when hunting over bait or with hounds. The problem is that the scope has to be mounted slightly higher in order to see the open sights beneath it, which usually means you have to lift your head slightly to use the scope or jam your cheek into the rifle stock to use the open sights. Either way, getting proper sight alignment can be difficult. The nice thing about most bear hunting situations, however, is that the hunter often has time to make the necessary adjustments. Still, I'd recommend sticking with one sight or the other.

Learn to shoot with both eyes open when using a scope, especially at close range. The non-shooting eye will concentrate on the whole picture before you while the shooting eye centers on the target. This not only increases accuracy but also speed.

At close range, open sights and aperture or peeps sights are adequate for bear hunting. But unless the hunter is an excellent shot they should be limited to under a hundred yards or so. They simply offer too much room for error, and at long range it's difficult to locate the vitals. I prefer peep sights because the aperture on the rear sight helps you align with the front sight much quicker. Your eyes just naturally flows to the front sight. Aperture sights typically come with interchangeable eyepieces, with different sized holes in each. A smaller hole is best for sighting in, but when practicing and hunting, go with the larger opening, which seems to bring more light to the eye and allows for faster alignment, almost as fast as some scopes at low power.

While you often hear it said that open sights are faster than scopes at close range, the opposite is most often true. You can simply see better through a scope, not only when picking out the

Open sights are fine for taking black bears at close range.

vitals, but in low-light conditions. On the other hand, open sights and peep sights do have an advantage over scopes in wet weather, particularly during a downpour or snowstorm.

It's possible to kill a bear with some extremely light calibers if the bullet hits the right spot. I have seen it done more than once. On the other hand, you can whollop a bruin in the wrong place with the most powerful cartridge on the market and it may still limp away, never to be found. Unfortunately, I have seen this done all too often.

SHOT PLACEMENT

Let's take a look at the best places to target a black bear, and at some of the best shot angles. Bears are no different than other big game in the sense that the deadliest shot is to the brain or spinal cord in the neck. A solid shot to either area will put a black bear down hard and keep it there. However, this doesn't mean that these are necessarily good shots to take.

For one thing, the skull of a black bear has some of the thickest, strongest bone on the entire animal. Although larger than the skulls on some other North American big game, it's fairly small in comparison to the vitals area, even on the largest boars. The skull of an average bear only measures about eleven inches long by six to seven inches wide, and the critical area that houses the brain is even smaller. For a good shooter this can offer a decent target at close range, but a difficult one at long range. Either way, the bone is so dense that a shot must be perfectly dead-on or it will literally bounce off. And it takes a powerful charge and proper bullet configuration to penetrate bone to the brain. A last-second flinch by the hunter, or even a slight shift by the animal, may cause the bullet to hit high or low, too far forward or back.

The spinal cord in the neck is also a small target, perhaps two or three inches in diameter, even on big boars. It must be severed completely to keep a bear on the ground. A neck shot that hits too high will result in a painful flesh wound that could get infected and cause permanent damage; too low may damage the windpipe, causing a slow, agonizing death.

Head and neck shots are just too risky most of the time. Not to mention the fact that a shot to the head ruins the skull for possible record-book contention. I usually avoid such fancy shooting in the field. In most cases, it's more luck than skill. I have too much respect for the animals I hunt to take the chance of wounding them when I can drop them quickly and cleanly with a safer shot to the vitals.

This means the lung and heart area. A black bear taken through the lungs is a dead bear, pure and simple. It may dash off a short distance, but it won't go far, often less than fifty yards and rarely over a hundred. The lungs cover a good portion of the forward third of the bear's body. They are by far the biggest target. Also, the heart is between the lungs, the aorta is at the top of the heart, and the liver and kidneys are behind them. Hit any of these organs well and you'll quickly kill your bear. A shot to this area offers the widest room for error. If you hit too high, there's still a good chance of hitting the spinal cord, which will also put a bear down.

The best angle into the lungs is perfectly broadside. A broadside shot, even from elevated stands, requires the least amount of penetration and is the most direct route into the lungs. It's the one shot I take whenever possible, and when it's not available I often wait for it.

There is much debate among hunters about whether to hit a black bear directly in the lungs or to break the near shoulder on the way in. The option is yours. Both work extremely well, but demolishing the shoulder first and then continuing into the lungs can really anchor a bear—provided the load has sufficient energy and is of the right design to break bone and still penetrate well. Some hunters even believe it is best to break the near shoulder, continue into the lungs, and break the far shoulder, but to be honest I've never done this and see no need for it. If you prefer lighter loads, a shot directly into the lungs will do just fine.

The key is to find the right aiming point. Locating the shoulder is rarely a problem, except under low-light conditions, but even then a scope makes the job relatively easy. A bear's shoulder is slightly more forward than deer and other hoofed game, and forms a tighter angle, so the proper aiming point for a shoulder hit is also a bit more forward. If you want a direct hit to the lungs, aim slightly back, following a line along the middle of the near leg to a point about a third to halfway up the chest. Depending on the way a bear is positioned, the shoulder blade acts like a plate of armor over much of the lungs, so wait for the forward leg to move slightly ahead of the body, if possible.

This broadside angle is perfect for a clean lung/heart shot.

If you wait until this bear steps forward—moving the near foreleg in front of the body—you'll have a better chance of hitting the vitals.

The perfect broadside shot is not always possible; in fact, it's a blessing when you get it. Many shots at black bears are at an angle, quartering away or toward the hunter. The more severe the angle on a quartering-away shot, the greater the chance of hitting the animal too far back. The less a bear angles away, the closer you are to making the easier broadside shot. When a bear is lined up at a slight angle, locate the front shoulder and pick a point just behind it, imagining a line from this point through the opposite shoulder.

As the angle increases, a shot slightly farther back from the near shoulder is better—perhaps just a couple of inches or so, or even to the back of the ribs on a sharp angle. Think three dimensionally. Visualize where the lungs are, and don't aim too far back or you'll hit the paunch. When the angle gets very sharp, don't take the shot.

Bears quartering toward you are always tricky because the head and shoulder blade block a portion of the vitals. Again, picture where the lungs are. On an animal that's closer to broadside, a shot just behind the front shoulder is still the best option, but as the angle increases, a shot in front of the shoulder might be better. If the angle is really sharp, you might have to shift the aiming point to the neck.

Head-on shots are tough, too, because the head provides a greater level of protection and the projectile can be easily deflected. When a bear is coming right at you, the lungs are at the base of the neck between the shoulders, offering a much smaller target area. A hunter using a centerfire rifle and scope can make the shot, but only when the neck or chest area is exposed. But when a bear is standing on two legs (facing you) for a better look around or sitting with its head up, the shot is much easier. The chest is fully exposed, and a shot directly into the chest a few inches below the neck is deadly. There is also some room for error here, since lungs are quite wide from this view, but try to place your shot near the middle of the chest.

Rear-end shots should always be avoided. A black bear is compact and well muscled. Very few high-powered rifles and bullets have what it takes to penetrate the full length of a bear, plowing through the intestines and paunch before reaching the lungs.

One of my favorite shot opportunities, especially from elevated stands over bait, is when the bear is sitting or standing on all fours with its back to me. I prefer the bear to be sitting because the back is more erect, but either way, a shot directly into the middle of the shoulder blades will break the spine, killing the animal almost instantly. I took two of my largest boars in Alberta with this shot. Both measured well over six feet, and both simply collapsed without moving an inch.

For firearm hunters, shooting from elevated stands is only slightly different from level shots. The more the height of a stand increases, the more the position of the backbone and shoulder blade in relation to the vitals changes. A steeper angle means that more of the lung area is protected, which decreases the target area in the vitals. This is why I don't like stands above twelve to fifteen feet high, especially over bait at close range.

SELECTING A CALIBER AND CARTRIDGE

When selecting a centerfire caliber and cartridge for black bears, it's important to match the gun to the style of hunting. Some rifles are too heavy or cumbersome to tote on long jaunts, even with a sling. These rifles usually shoot extremely well and help absorb recoil, but they can be difficult to hold steady, particularly on long-range shots. It's probably best to leave them at home on spot-and-stalk hunts or when chasing hounds over hills or through dense cover. Even on stand, they can be difficult to maneuver and hold on target as you wait for the best angle.

Lightweight rifles are usually good shooters, too. Some are shorter than standard rifles, making them good choices on long stalks or when following hounds, and their short length and low weight make them easy to handle and maneuver in stands. But they do seem to have a bit more recoil, which may cause a hunter who hasn't practiced shooting regularly to flinch in anticipation just as the trigger is pulled.

Many rifles offer a happy medium, but it's a decision only the hunter can make based on his personal preferences and method of hunting black bears. The rifle you already own and use regularly for deer-sized game may just be the rifle you need for black bears.

The generally accepted rule of thumb is that it takes about 1,000 foot-pounds of energy to dispatch deer-sized game, and

Many popular bear guns now sport synthetic stocks, which are lighter and stand up well to harsh conditions.

2,000 foot-pounds for elk-sized game. I more or less agree with that, although a bear can certainly be dispatched with less energy when properly hit in the vitals at certain ranges. The vulnerable .30–30 is a prime example. In the East, the average shot is only around fifty or sixty yards. Here, the .30–30 has undoubtedly taken more deer than any other caliber, yet it's not considered a long-range killing machine because it loses too much energy.

When loaded with a 170-grain bullet, the .30–30 delivers just over 1,800 foot-pounds of energy, but at a hundred yards this falls off to just over 1,300 foot-pounds. This is enough to kill small or medium-sized bears when properly hit, but not by much. Cut the range in half, to around fifty or sixty yards, and the .30–30 works quite well.

In the West, where the average shot distance is greater, the .30–30 just doesn't cut it most of the time. Keep in mind that the

This Alberta bruin was taken with a .444 Marlin firing a 265-grain bullet. This combination is best for shots under a hundred yards.

caliber is merely the diameter of the bullet, and it has little to do with energy or velocity. It does, however, determine the size of the wound channel and the amount of internal damage on impact. The .30–30 creates a fairly small wound channel; certainly enough to down a bear that's solidly hit in the lungs, but without the downrange killing power Western hunters need.

To a point, velocity is a good thing. It helps flatten trajectory, which makes aiming and shooting easier at long range. But when hunting over bait or with hounds, where close shots are the norm, great velocity isn't so critical, although it does help deliver shock to an animal. Too much speed is not always a good thing because it can create premature expansion of the bullet, and with some bullets controllability above 3,000 feet per second becomes a problem.

Bullet velocity and resistance, which in this case is the body tissue of an animal, helps determine bullet expansion. The black bear is heavily and densely muscled, so a bullet with too much velocity can be just as much of a disadvantage as a bullet traveling at a slower velocity. In general, the best black bear guns have a muzzle velocity between 2,200 and 2,400 feet per second. Even at 200 to 300 yards, most popular bullets within this range will be clipping along fast enough to allow good penetration and proper expansion.

More important than velocity is power—how much energy a bullet delivers, not at the muzzle, but where it counts, at impact. I could care less how much energy a bullet has at the muzzle, but I'll take all I can get downrange. Energy is dictated in part by velocity, but also by bullet weight. Basically, if a heavy bullet can retain velocity downrange, it will deliver more energy on impact than lighter counterparts of the same caliber, even if they're traveling faster.

There are exceptions, of course. A 150-grain load from a .30–06 smacks into an animal with just over 1,700 foot-pounds of energy at 200 yards, yet a 180-grain bullet in the same gun delivers about 1,630 ft-lbs at this range. In the middle is the 165-grain bullet, which hits just over 2,000 ft-lbs. The 180-grain bullet has a slower muzzle velocity, slows more quickly en route, and is traveling slower at 200 yards than the 150-grain bullet. The 165-grain, on the other hand, leaves the muzzle slightly slower than the 150-grain, but better retains its velocity, and therefore its energy, downrange.

Even at 400 yards, the 165-grain bullet hits with over 1,950 ft-lbs of energy, while energy from the 150-grain and 180-grain bullets has dropped off to about 1,700 and 1,460 ft-lbs, respectively. So while all three

A .30-06 shooting a 165-grain bullet took this fine Newfoundland bear. It has good penetration and power out to 200 yards or more.

bullets will dispatch a black bear at long range, the 165-grain is the best choice simply because it retains more energy downrange than the other two.

Shots at close range are another matter. It's possible to have too much of a good thing, both in terms of energy and velocity. When taking fifty- or sixty-yard shots over bait or with hounds, the 150-grain in .30–06 is the better choice. The heavier bullets sometimes penetrate completely through a black bear, or end up against the skin on the far side, perhaps not even completely expanding, which wastes a lot of their energy. The 150-grain bullet will usually fully mushroom at this range, exerting all its energy inside the bear where it counts.

So in long-range shooting situations, always go with bullet weight over muzzle velocity. Out to three hundred yards or so, the velocity differs only slightly in most cases, but the energy

This small Maine bear was taken with a .30-06, one of the most popular calibers for black bears.

retained is considerable. At close range, under a hundred yards, cutting back on weight is usually okay.

Bullet shape also plays a role. Most big game cartridges are now available in round-nose, flat- or snub-nose, hollowpoint, and aerodynamic spitzer designs. For shots beyond a couple hundred yards, the sharp-pointed spitzer bullets are a good choice because they cut through the air much easier and retain velocity and energy extremely well. But they travel so fast, even at long range, that unless they hit bone spitzers have a tendency to travel straight through soft tissue, leaving a small wound channel. The bear will still die if hit well, but you may have to do some tracking after the shot.

The round-nose, or even flat-nose, cartridges often work just as well or better, particularly at close range. They retain good speed and energy, but their rounded or flattened configurations allow them to mushroom well inside the animal, causing a great deal of shock and large wound channels. They also do an excel-

The author's brother, Dave, used a 7mm to bag this Manitoba bear.

lent job on bone, passing right through it and into the vitals with the right caliber and energy.

Although some bear hunters disagree, I usually stay away from hollowpoint bullets on black bears because of their tendency to open too quickly and not penetrate far, especially on bone. The counter argument is that a high-velocity hollowpoint bullet will create a larger wound channel, therefore creating more blood loss, and more shock. The theory makes sense, but in my experience it doesn't always work this way. When I hit bone I want full penetration into the vitals, and depending on the circumstances, hollowpoints often fail to do this.

In the end, you'll have to choose your cartridge based on the type of country you'll be hunting in and how far you expect to shoot.

The following is a list of popular rifle calibers and bullet weights that I consider adequate for black bears at various ranges. These recommendations are based on personal experience and the opinions of others in the business who have been hunting black bears as long, if not longer, than I have. Of course, there are no absolutes. Knowing what a particular cartridge is capable of at various ranges and matching a selection with your method of hunting takes experience and research, but the guidelines below should provide a good starting point.

RECOMMENDED SHOOTING DISTANCE

Cartridge	Bullet Weight (Grains)	100 Yards	200 Yards	300+Yards
.264 Win. Mag.	140	x	x	
.270 Win.	150	x	x	
.270 Win. Mag.	150	x	x	
7mm–08 Rem.	140	x		
7x57	140	x		
7x57	175	x	x	
.284 Win.	150	x	x	

Cartridge	Bullet Weight (Grains)	100 Yards	200 Yards	300+Yards
.280 Rem.	140	x		
.280 Rem.	175	x	x	
7mm Rem. Mag.	150	x	x	
7mm Rem. Mag.	175	x	x	x
7mm Wby. Mag.	150	x	x	
7mm Wby. Mag.	175	x	x	x
.30–30 Win.	170	x		
.307 Win.	150	x		
.307 Win.	180	x	x	
.308 Win	150	x		
.308 Win.	180	x	x	
.30–06 Spr.	150	x	x	
.30–06 Spr.	165	x	x	x
.30–06 Spr.	180	x	x	x
.300 Win. Mag.	180	x	x	x
.300 Win. Mag.	200	x	x	x
.300 Wby. Mag.	180	x	x	x
.300 Wby. Mag.	220	x	x	x
8mm Rem. Mag.	185	x	x	x
8mm Rem. Mag.	220	x	x	x
.338 Win. Mag.	200	x	x	x
.338 Win. Mag.	225	x	x	x
.338 Win. Mag.	250	x	x	x
.340 Wby. Mag.	200	x	x	x
.340 Wby. Mag.	250	x	x	x
.348 Win.	200	x	x	
.35 Rem.	200	x		
.358 Win.	200	x	x	
.356 Win.	200	x	x	
.356 Win.	250	x	x	
.35 Whelen	200	x	x	
.35 Whelen	250	x	x	
.350 Rem. Mag.	200	x	x	
.375 Win.	200	x		
.375 Win.	250	x		
.375 H&H Mag.	270	x	x	x
.375 H&H Mag.	300	x	x	x
.378 Wby. Mag.	270	x	x	x
.378 Wby. Mag.	300	x	x	x
.44 Mag.	240	x		
.444 Marlin	240	x		
.444 Marlin	265	x		
.45–70 Govt.	300	x		
.45–70 Govt.	405	x		

Chapter

5

BOWHUNTING

I'll admit up front that I'm not the most avid bowhunter. It's not that I dislike bowhunting; in fact, I own a couple of modern compounds and more arrows than I'll ever need (at least according to my wife). And I hunt with them regularly during special bow seasons. It's just that I'd rather hunt with a muzzleloader when possible.

Archery fans often claim that taking big game with a bow and arrow is the ultimate hunting challenge. I have taken big game with every legal weapon on the books — modern rifle, handgun, bow, muzzleloader, and crossbow — and in my humble opinion they each have unique challenges. With the speed and sight systems of modern bows, aluminum and carbon arrows, improved releases, and other new contrivances, hunting at close range with today's compounds, even for black bears, is no more of a challenge than hunting with a muzzleloader. That statement is bound to raise some hackles, but I will stick by it. Of course, hunting with a recurve or longbow, without the aid of fancy fiberoptic sights and all the other paraphernalia normally associated with modern bowhunting, is an entirely different matter.

Over the years, I've taken several species with a bow, including three black bears using a compound and aluminum arrows.

The modern compound bow is a marvelous piece of hunting equipment. With proper shot placement, it can easily throw an arrow completely through a black bear.

Even with such top-of-the-line equipment, it's difficult for rifle hunters to get used to the limited range potential. I know hunters who are accurate on deer-sized game out to fifty or even sixty yards, but on black bears thirty to thirty-five yards is a long shot. This isn't because a modern compound bow lacks the ability to throw an arrow fast enough or with enough kinetic energy to penetrate into the vitals.

Both one- and two-cam bows, shooting arrows equipped with broadheads made with strong ferrules and scalpel-sharp blades, can easily handle the job at that range. Even a recurve bow or longbow with a draw weight over fifty pounds can kill a bear at a good distance. Some compound bows can unleash an arrow on a fairly flat trajectory at more than 300 feet per second, and though longbows and recurves are slower, perhaps 170 to 185 feet per second and 190 feet per second, respectively, all are more than capable of getting an arrow to a target over forty yards away in short order. And with the right arrow shaft and broadhead combination, there's usually enough speed and energy to kill a black bear at this distance.

The problem at longer range is shot placement. Without question, hitting the vitals with a killing shot is more difficult for archers, simply because there are few options available. Part of the reason is that an arrow works differently on game than a bullet. Broadheads are designed to cut, causing death through massive blood loss. The arrow must hit and penetrate an organ where this matters most. So the lungs are the only place to hit a bear with an arrow, and ideally it should be a double-lung shot.

As the lungs of a bear offer the largest target, hitting them sounds rather easy. But when you take into consideration the massive shoulder armor and thick leg bones, all of which an arrow won't penetrate, this important target area gets pretty small, even with a broadside shot. It gets even smaller on quartering-away and quartering-in shots, perhaps half the original target size, depending on the angle.

A broadside lung shot requires the least amount of penetration, and this should be the primary goal of all archers pursuing black bears. It's also the best angle for a double-lung shot, which usu-

Shot placement is always critical in bowhunting. This color-phase bear was taken in Alberta.

ally collapses at least one lung and sometimes both. A quick death is the result. The big worry is hitting too far back. As discussed in the previous chapter, a bear's shoulder is slightly more forward than a deer's, and the shoulder blade forms a tighter triangle, so the best aiming point when broadside is farther back — but not by much.

The aiming point can be found by following the center of the front leg upward to a point a third to halfway up the chest. Aim slightly behind this area to miss the shoulder. If the bear's near leg is slightly back or straight, wait until the bear moves it slightly forward before releasing the arrow. This will open up more of the chest.

A bear that is quartering away may also offer a good shot to the bowhunter, but the degree of the angle matters more than it does for rifle shooters. The more a bear is quartering away, the worse the shot, because an arrow has to penetrate farther to reach the lungs. And if it hits too far back, it'll stick in the intestines and paunch. Picture where the lungs are and aim accordingly. In some cases, it helps to use the far-side front leg to find the best aiming point. As the angle increases, the target area shrinks, so archers need to discipline themselves to pass on shots too far away from broadside. It's easy to miss too far back in an attempt to avoid hitting the shoulder.

Some other shots are almost always a no-no for the bowhunter. Head-on shots fall into this category. A bear often carries its head low when it walks, which puts the head in front of the lungs and heart. Even skilled archers should avoid this angle. In fact, any shot is risky when the bear is facing the archer, even if it's sitting down with a fully exposed chest. Bears positioned this way have a greater chance of spotting the archer as he draws and prepares to shoot. It should go without saying that a rear-end shot is out of the question. From straight away, or even from a slight angle, the vitals are simply protected by too much muscle, intestine, and paunch. You'll never get through to the lungs this way.

Shooting down from a stand can be tricky for the archer, too. Steeper shooting angles reduce the target size into the vitals, and the spine and shoulder blade shield more of the lungs. A double-lung shot is often more difficult to nail, as well, due to the closeness of the shot and downward angle. If you know you're going to be bowhunting during the season, place your stands to maximize your opportunities for a lung shot. And if you're planning to take a guided hunt, it's particularly important to inform the outfitter that you'll be using a bow so he can make the necessary adjustments.

If you don't think a double-lung shot is realistic, concentrate on hitting one lung as solidly as possible. You may still totally collapse the lung with a straight-through penetration of the arrow, if all bones are missed, and there's usually a good blood trail to follow. The bear isn't likely to travel very far anyway.

A fair shot for the archer is when the bear is sitting with its back fully exposed. By aiming between the shoulders, slightly off center in order to miss the backbone, the arrow will have a clear path into one of the lungs.

Keep in mind that when shooting downward you often must adjust the aiming point vertically depending on the angle and range, particularly if using slower longbows and recurves. When a bear is broadside, aim slightly high on the near side. The arrow will likely hit the closest lung and then enter the far lung on its continued downward trajectory, resulting is a double lunger. With the speed of today's modern compound bows and arrows, however, you can probably aim dead-on up to around thirty yards or so. If the stand is only twelve to fifteen feet off the ground, the trajectory of the arrow will have little, if any, drop at this range.

As with any type of shooting, it pays to practice from elevated stands prior to a hunt. If you're planning a spot-and-stalk hunt with a modern compound bow, practice out to around forty yards or so. That is a long shot at a black bear with a bow, and not all archers will be able to shoot accurately enough at this distance. Practice enough to know your limitations and discipline yourself to pass on shots that are likely to leave wounded game in the field. Accepting these limitations is one of the reasons hunters choose bows in the first place. And remember to practice shooting from a variety of positions, as you never know how you'll be situated when a shot opportunity presents itself.

Inexperienced bowhunters should use full-size 3-D targets, set up at different angles. I have an old bear target from McKenzie made of dense, flexible, self-closing foam that I even use when experimenting with rifle, handgun, muzzleloader, and slug guns. These targets are not intended for high-powered firearms of

When shooting from an elevated stand, it may be necessary to make an adjustment. The hunter looking down at this bear needs to wait for a better shot opportunity. (USFWS)

course, and mine is pretty well shot up, but I keep patching it with spray insulation and black paint and it manages to stay together.

Some 3-D targets even have removable and replaceable vitals sections. Just make sure to set up in a safe place or to use proper backstops and rid the area of any rocks and debris that might cause a ricochet. Full-size targets offer the best anatomical representation of what a real bear will look like on a bait.

SELECTING A BOW AND ARROWS

The most common type of bow in use today is the pulley- or cam-operated compound bow. These bows are largely responsible for the current popularity of bowhunting because they make things a whole lot easier. A compound bow offers several important advantages over a recurve or longbow. For one thing, it's easier to shoot heavy draw weights while holding the bow at full draw. With recurves and longbows, the pressure increases as the string is pulled back, with maximum tension at full draw. But compounds have the most tension at the start of the draw. At about the halfway point, the cams or pulleys allow the limbs to "break," or "roll over," reducing the amount of effort needed to reach full draw. When the arrow is released the pulleys or cams snap the limbs back to full draw strength.

The difference, or "let-off," between the initial draw weight and final holding weight on two-wheeled compounds can be as much 60 or 70 percent. Compounds that incorporate a pulley and cam may have a let-off of 75 to 80 percent. In either case, it's easier to hold at full draw for rather long periods of time, which is vital when you're waiting for the perfect shot. (Some states have a maximum allowable let-off, so check the regulations where you plan to hunt.)

Compound bows with pulleys are generally easier to draw than ones with cams, and many cam-operated compounds have

This PSE Fire Flight is a typical modern compound. It weighs just over three pounds, has a 70-percent let-off, and throws an arrow up to 294 feet per second.

to be drawn farther back before the bow "breaks." But they typically provide more arrow speed, more power, and deeper penetration when set at the same poundage as their wheeled counterparts. Some modified compounds that use cams are also referred to as "overdraw" bows, because they actually have to be overdrawn before they break, or let off. Both styles are highly efficient and make excellent choices for bear hunting, providing greater arrow speed and flatter trajectories than recurves or longbows.

It should be noted, though, that overdraw bows are better at shooting shorter, lighter arrows, which fly much faster and have flatter trajectories. To accommodate the shorter arrows, the arrow rest is moved farther back behind the sight window, which takes some getting used to. For this reason, and due to the lighter arrows and faster speeds, it's necessary to use some kind of mechanical release with these bows.

Compounds also allow the user to adjust the draw weight. My PSE Nova Extreme can be adjusted between fifty and sixty pounds, but other bows offer an even wider range of adjustment depending on bow length. This lets the archer gradually build up from a low pull weight to maximum pull without having to switch bows. The shooter becomes more comfortable with the bow in the process.

For black bears, a draw weight of fifty-five to sixty pounds, regardless of the bow type, is usually considered best. Some archers prefer more, but it really isn't needed. PSE, Hoyt, Darton, Bear, Browning, Martin, Mathews, McPherson, Oneida, American Archery, Alpine, Tri-SECTRA, Golden, Champion, and High Country all make high-quality compound bows.

Overall weight is also worth considering when you buy a compound bow. The trend these days seems to be toward lighter bows, those under three pounds. These are nice for packing or when chasing hounds, but lightweight bows don't seem to be as accurate as slightly heavier bows. As a general rule, heavier bows are more stable. One weighing around four pounds or so is a good place to start.

Longer compound bows are generally easier to draw. My favorite compound measures 37½ inches axle-to-axle, but some run as little as 31 inches. Although the current trend seems to be toward shorter bows, the longer one suits me. I can pull it to full draw while sitting, kneeling, or standing, and hold it steady.

Traditional longbows and recurve bows are making a comeback of sorts among archers looking to simplify things. While most modern compounds are set up with elaborate pin or fiberoptic sight systems, stabilizers, fancy arrow rests, bow quivers, and other gadgets, shooting a longbow or recurve is more basic, more instinctive. They present more of a challenge for archers because the shooter's skills must be that much sharper, and also because they throw arrows at slower speeds.

Longbows, the slower of the two, are roughly seventy to eighty inches in length. Recurve bows are faster because the entire bow is shorter, usually from fifty to sixty-five inches or so, and because the limbs bend inward at a sharper angle then outward at the tips. Longer recurves are easier to draw, shoot smoother, and throw arrows faster than shorter ones. Something in the sixty-inch class is a good choice for hunting.

It can be awkward to get a longbow into shooting position when hunting from an elevated stand, recurves less so. Some recurve bows are available in break-down models, which makes them easier to carry into a stand or when following dogs, and some can be equipped with stabilizers, bow quivers, even sights. There's a lot less to traditional bows than compounds, which means there is less that can go wrong. However, because longbows and recurves usually require more skill to shoot accurately and consistently, they aren't recommended for novice hunters, particularly those tackling black bears for the first time.

A quality traditional bow isn't exactly cheap, either. Handcrafted or custom models are just as expensive, if not more so, than a good quality compound. If you are a beginning bowhunter, I'd recommend starting with a compound with pulleys, jumping up to cam and overdrawn counterparts as your experience and skills increase.

When selecting a compound bow, it's important to first know your draw length. Hold a yardstick on the center of your chest and parallel to the floor. Extend your arms outward along the yardstick. The measurement at the end of your fingertips is your draw length. While arrows of the same approximate length are the general rule, they should also match the draw weight of your bow. Charts to help you with this are available from Easton, a major arrow manufacturer, and are usually available through retailers. Make sure you know the holding weight at full draw and at peak weight before you buy arrows to match.

This may sound complicated, but it really isn't. Most hunters buy their bow and arrows at the same store, and a reputable dealer will assemble the outfit for you, taking your draw length and recommending draw weight and suitable arrows.

A lot of archers go with too much draw weight, starting out at sixty pounds or more with heavy arrows, evidently thinking that the more power and speed, the better. While the latter is true, more poundage often sacrifices accuracy. Any modern compound drawing at fifty to fifty-five pounds will put a properly placed arrow right through a black bear, and by using lighter arrows you'll maintain a good trajectory without sacrificing accuracy. The draw should be one smooth movement, and there's no sense in using a bow that you have to fight with. You need to be able to reach full draw without raising the bow or putting much effort into it, so find a draw weight that lets you do this and stick with it.

For years, the most popular arrows for compound bows were made of aluminum, and these arrows still remain a top choice. They are lightweight, strong, consistent in diameter, and work very well on black bears. They are also available in different weights, or grains, to match the draw weight of the bow used, and in some cases even the animal being hunted. Bear hunters used to prefer heavier arrows, but the truth is that even lighter arrows provide great penetration these days, as well as great speed and a flat trajectory.

A good rule of thumb when considering arrow weight is go with five grains of arrow weight for each pound of bow weight. Simply multiply the pull weight by five. For example, if your bow has a fifty-pound pull, go with an arrow no less than 250 grains. If your bow is set at fifty-five pounds, go with an arrow no less than 275 grains. Chances are, you won't have to go any higher.

Aluminum arrow weight is determined by the diameter of the shaft and the thickness of the shaft wall. These measurements are clearly marked on each shaft and are consistent from manufacturer to manufacturer. I currently shoot Easton Gamegetter II 2216 arrows, and have had good luck with them on black bears and deer-sized game. The first two numbers (22) give the outside diameter in sixty-fourths of an inch, while the second two numbers (16) indicate the wall thickness in thousandths of an inch.

In recent years, carbon arrows have become popular. When first introduced, splintering was a problem, but they've come a long way since then. Today, carbon arrows are as strong and consistent as aluminum shafts, and reputedly just as durable. Unfortunately, carbon arrows are not marked the same as aluminum arrows, and there is no uniformity within the industry. One manufacturer may mark them 45/70, which basically means that arrow can be used with bows having a draw weight of forty-five to seventy pounds. Other manufacturers may use a completely different designation—2300, 2400, or 2500, for example, or some other series of numbers. In general, the smaller the number, the lighter the arrow. If in doubt, ask a reputable dealer to help match the right arrow to your bow.

Aluminum or carbon, you can't go wrong when using a compound bow. The bottom line is that you need to match the arrow to your bow and practice enough to become comfortable, consistent, and accurate.

Traditional longbow enthusiasts still prefer arrows made of cedar, while recurve users can select between fiberglass, aluminum, or carbon.

Plastic vanes and real feathers are both available as fletching, and each has its good and bad points. Plastic vanes are waterproof, but feathers are a bit more forgiving, although they can be noisy on the release or if brushed against something. I have also had feathers shoot off a shaft upon release, but this may have been more my fault than the arrow's. Still, this rarely happens with plastic vanes.

What is on the other end of the arrow actually matters a lot more. Broadheads are the standard tip for all big game. It is imperative that any broadhead be razor-sharp, made of the best steel, and have stout ferrules. The two major types are fixed blade, which must be sharpened after use, and replaceable, which come pre-sharpened and can be swapped out as needed. I prefer pre-sharpened, replaceable-blade broadheads simply because I hate taking the time to sharpen the other kind. But even with pre-sharpened broadheads, I make sure to test the sharpness before hunting, touching them up with a special tool specifically designed for that purpose. Fortunately, it's rarely necessary.

Broadheads come with two, three, or four cutting edges, and in different grains. For black bears, I like a four-blade broadhead because it usually provides a slightly larger cutting diameter, although some three-blade broadheads are nearly as large. I also like a broadhead in the 130- to 145-grain range for my bow. They fly fast and flat and have great penetration. You shouldn't go any lighter than 100- to 115-grain for bears, but the most important aspect is matching the arrow and broadhead to your particular bow.

The arrow that killed this Manitoba bear was tipped with a Muzzy three-blade 125-grain broadhead, a good choice for black bears.

Compound bows are usually equipped with quivers that aid with balance and keep arrows handy. This bear was taken in Alberta.

New Archery Products, Muzzy, Rocket, Montec, Steel Forge, Satellite Archery, Wasp, Rocky Mountain, Barrie Archery, Golden-Key Futura, GameTracker, AHT, Archer's Ammo, Elk Mountain Archery, Zwickey, Delta, and Magnus offer broadheads of high quality that work well on black bears when fitted to the right shaft and bow.

A few other items will be helpful when bowhunting. Quivers can be carried on the back or attached directly to the bow. Most compound hunters, and some recurve users, use bow-mounted quivers. I prefer this kind because it seems to help balance the bow and keeps extra arrows handy. Traditional longbow hunters usually carry over-the-back quivers.

A glove, tab, or mechanical release is also required. A lot of compound hunters, especially those with cam and overdraw bows, like a mechanical release, but I prefer a tab for my two-pulley compound. (A tab helps keep finger pressure off the nock.) I still shoot well with a glove, though, and use one from time to time. There should be a nocking point on the bowstring, and many compounds these days come with them. They should be properly positioned one-eighth to a half-inch above a point at a ninety-degree angle above the arrow rest.

Other options include an armguard, bowstring silencers, and some kind of sight system for those not shooting instinctively. Sev-

A bowhunter killed this bear in Idaho. Some states now offer special bow-only hunting seasons for black bears.

eral types of sights are available: peep, pin, pendulum, laser, fiber optic, even scopes. For bears, fiber-optic sights are great because they help you find the pin sight under low-light conditions.

BOW-ONLY BEAR HUNTING SEASONS

State or Province	Season Dates*
Alaska	varies
Arizona	March–May and August–October
Arkansas	October
California	August–September
Georgia	September–October
Idaho	August–October
Michigan	October
New Mexico	September
New York	September–October (north) and October–December (south)
Tennessee	Fall
Utah	August–September
Virginia	October–November
West Virginia	October–November
Wisconsin	September
Wyoming	April and August
Manitoba	May–June and September
New Brunswick	September
Newfoundland/Labrador	September–November

*Season availability and dates may change. Hunters should check the latest state/provincial hunting regulations summary for details. Some seasons only apply to specific counties, and special licenses and permits may be required for certain archery hunts.

Chapter

6

MUZZLELOADERS AND SLUG GUNS

MUZZLELOADERS

I killed my first black bear with a muzzleloader. The gun, still one of my favorites, was a Lyman Great Plains Rifle in .54 caliber with a 1:66 twist. I chose it for the hunt because of its larger bore size and ability to throw a heavier roundball. I had read an article that stated bigger was always better when using roundballs in muzzleloaders. Although a .50-caliber gun loaded with a .490-inch, 177-grain ball might do the trick, a heavier 225-grain projectile would retain good speed and energy out to seventy yards or so, creating a large wound channel. The author seemed to know what he was talking about, and as I was planning to hunt over bait, with the shot at only twenty yards or so, it all made sense. The bear was no monster, but I took it with a single well-placed shot that literally dropped it on the spot. The rug is now on the floor in my office.

In those days, muzzleloading enthusiasts had little to choose from in terms of rifle design, projectiles, and propellant. Round-ball guns, either sidelock percussion or flintlock, were more popular than they are today, and along with a few models rifled with a 1:48 twist—designed to shoot roundballs, maxi-balls, and other solid lead conicals—they were about the only ones available.

Blackpowder was the propellant of choice because it was the only propellant on the market. The in-line muzzleloader was still a long way off, and there were no saboted pistol bullets, no fiber-optic sight systems, and scopes were rarely seen. Pyrodex, Clear-Shot, Triple-Seven, and other propellant substitutes, granular or pellet, had not even been conceived. Hunters carried everything with them: propellant, generally in a powder flask of some sort; priming powder, if using a flintlock; measurer; projectiles; patches, if necessary; and caps, if using a percussion model—all in a pouch or "possibles bag." There were no quick-loaders, no fancy cappers, none of the little gadgets now available that make life as a blackpowder hunter much easier.

Hunting black bears and other big game with muzzleloaders grew in popularity along with all of the technological advances over the last couple of decades. In general, muzzleloaders are

great bear guns, but the type and size of projectile, the amount of propellant used, and how you plan to hunt black bears are major factors in how well your gun will perform.

Let's start by taking a look at the three basic igni-

This .50-caliber Pennsylvania flintlock long rifle is designed to shoot a patch and roundball.

tion systems: flintlock, percussion, and in-line. Flintlock and percussion models were among the earliest designs. These guns are generally referred to as sidelock muzzleloaders because the hammer that strikes the initial primer, either a percussion cap or priming powder located in a pan called a frizzen, is literally on the side of the lock system.

When the trigger is pulled, sparks from the initial priming charge or cap are sent into the main powder charge. The primary ignition charge must travel a short distance in order to reach the breech. Sparks from a percussion cap actually have to turn a ninety-degree corner to reach the breech, while sparks from a flintlock travel directly into the breech from the priming pan. The ignition on percussion muzzleloaders is almost instantaneous, so slight that it's often barely detectable. The flintlock system, however, is much slower because the priming powder must ignite before sparking and igniting the charge in the breech. There is typically a flash of the priming powder, a slight delay, then the ignition of the main charge.

The flintlock's priming powder is also exposed, simply sitting in the priming pan. It's covered by the frizzen, which affords some degree of protection, but the priming charge on a flintlock is more exposed to the air and elements around it than a percussion

Of the three primary muzzleloader designs, the flintlock is the slowest and least reliable, although it has been used successfully on black bears since colonial times.

Sidelock percussion muzzleloaders offer more speed than flintlocks and most accommodate a variety of projectiles.

cap, which is fully incased. Although I have experienced few problems with flintlocks, its ignition system is generally considered less reliable, particularly in wet weather. Because it's faster and better protected, the percussion system is more popular these days.

Both designs remain in use, though, and since the arrival of the early colonists, the flintlock and then the percussion, also known as the caplock, have taken their share of game large and small, including black bears. I own several modern caplock reproduction muzzleloaders from Thompson/Center, Connecticut Valley Arms (CVA), Traditions, and others, and I use them regularly on bear hunts. Probably half the black bears I've killed were taken with a sidelock muzzleloader.

Obviously, I like traditional muzzleloaders. More importantly, I understand and accept their limitations and hunt within those parameters. For example, some of today's replica flintlock

The Thompson/Center Hawken is one of the most popular replica percussion muzzle-loaders available today. It's rifled for roundballs and conical bullets.

muzzleloaders are manufactured with a slow rifle twist, generally 1:66, specifically designed for a patch and roundball only. But some flintlocks, and most caplocks, such as my Thompson/Center Custom Hawken, are built with a 1:48 twist. These guns shoot roundballs well, but because of the faster rate of twist, they'll also accommodate conical loads, even saboted bullets.

While a conical bullet from a caplock muzzleloader retains more energy farther downrange than a roundball, its trajectory is poor and proper shot placement difficult due to its rate of drop. A roundball is even less efficient, slowing and losing energy more quickly. Although both projectiles will kill black bears, roundball shooters are limited to around sixty- or seventy-yard shots and conical shooters to a hundred yards or so. But at those ranges, shot placement is crucial.

The modern in-line muzzleloader is the final type. There are two primary designs available: the plunger or striker style, which basically has a mechanism that slides forward to strike the percussion cap when the trigger is pulled, and the bolt-action, which works the same way but with a more powerful spring that allows the internal striker to travel a shorter distance much faster.

Both designs offer extremely fast ignition. The percussion cap, or a larger and hotter 209 shotgun primer, sits directly behind the breech, much closer to the main powder charge than flintlock or caplock models. Also, the striker, or bolt, travels a much shorter distance to the cap when the trigger is pulled, which allows the spark to go directly to the main charge. In a nutshell, the striker, nipple and cap, and main charge are all "in line." The short distance between striker and cap and then cap spark and main charge make ignition nearly instantaneous.

This makes the in-line muzzleloader extremely popular among hunters looking for improved performance. But there are other reasons for this popularity, as well. These guns look and fit like modern centerfire rifles, so hunters quickly feel comfortable with them. Most have removable breeches that are easy to clean, and more and more in-lines are being built on synthetic stocks, often camouflaged, which require little or no maintenance. They can easily be equipped with scopes, but if not, most come from the factory with fiber-optic sight systems. Because of their design, the nipple and cap on bolt-action models are also fully protected from the elements, and other in-lines have covers that offer solid protection. All of this makes the in-line a fast, reliable firearm.

Even more important for big game hunters, though, is that in-line muzzleloaders are designed with fast rifle twists: 1:28, 1:30, or 1:32. In-line guns are not inherently more accurate, nor do they shoot a great deal faster, flatter, or harder than a flintlock or sidelock percussion muzzleloader, but their elongated bullets have certain advantages when shot from a barrel with a fast rate of twist. Elongated bullets are heavier than roundballs and re-

The author took this record-book bear in northern Idaho using a modern in-line loaded with two 50-grain Pyrodex pellets and a 300-grain jacketed bullet.

quire more spin from faster rifling to keep them in the air. In-line muzzleloaders provide that spin. Conical lead bullets and jacketed bullets used with sabots are better at long range because they are more coefficient. This means they slice through the air better and retain more speed and energy downrange, making in-line muzzleloaders a better choice for distance shooting.

From a purely ballistic perspective, nothing is less efficient as it travels through the air than a roundball. Because it's round, and therefore pushes a lot of air, it slows down fairly quickly. It also drops quickly, which affects trajectory. For example, a .54-caliber roundball leaves the muzzle at between 1,700 and 1,800 feet per second (fps). That is pretty fast, but by the time it gets out to a hundred yards its velocity has dropped off to less than 700 fps or so.

Roundballs are also relatively light projectiles. Depending on actual diameter and lead composition, a .50-caliber roundball only weighs about 175 grains, the larger .54 roundball about 225 grains. That still has plenty of heft, even for black bears, but the important thing is how much energy it delivers to the target. Leaving the muzzle, the .54 caliber might have 2,000 foot-pounds of energy, which again is plenty, but by the time it gets a hundred yards downrange energy has dropped to less than 700 ft-lbs—perhaps just enough to kill a small black bear with perfect shot placement. The smaller .50-caliber roundball delivers even less punch.

Large-caliber roundballs are best for black bears because they're heavier and deliver more power. A .50-caliber roundball (left) and a .54 are shown here.

At under fifty yards, however, both the .50- and .54-caliber muzzleloaders shoot roundballs with manageable trajectories and enough speed and energy to kill a bear when hit properly. The larger .54-caliber gun is better, because the roundball is larger and heavier, and therefore hits harder at this range. Basically, roundball muzzleloaders are short-range guns, excellent for bait hunting or hunting with hounds.

To make heavier roundballs, you have to increase their diameter, or caliber, and it is diameter that determines their worthiness for big game. So in theory, a .58-caliber ball, or even a .60-caliber ball, would be better. But it takes a great deal of powder to get even minimally acceptable ballistics from these calibers, and speed and trajectory are sacrificed more quickly.

If you already own a .50-caliber roundball gun, it's fine to use on black bears—just keep the shot under fifty yards, closer if possible. But if you have a choice, go with the larger .54 caliber. Even then, keep your shot under seventy yards or so.

Within these range limits, the roundball is a good killer of black bears. This is because it offers excellent cohesiveness, meaning it holds together well upon impact. It also mushrooms extremely well. A .50-caliber roundball might open up to the size of a nickel, a .54-caliber roundball even more. This creates one hell of a wound channel, particularly in the lung area.

Conical and modern jacketed bullets have far different properties. Because they are elongated, it's possible to put more weight into the bullet by making it longer, while still maintaining caliber. For example, the Hornady Great Plains bullet, a favorite solid lead conical of mine, comes in .45, .50, and .54 caliber. The .45-caliber bullet weighs in at 285 grains, substantially more than a .54-caliber roundball, and the .50-caliber bullet at 385 grains, more than twice as much as a roundball. The .54 Plains bullet weighs 425 grains, 200 grains more than the .54-caliber roundball. Even jacketed pistol bullets used with sabots have more weight. And this extra weight translates into more energy downrange.

A 385-grain, .50-caliber conical in front of 120 grains of Pyrodex RS might leave the barrel at 1,500 fps and have 1,900 ft-lbs of energy. The same conical in .54 caliber might leave slightly faster at 1,550 fps and have 2,300 ft-lbs of energy. But at a hundred yards both are still clipping right along, still delivering 1,150 and 1,450 ft-lbs, respectively. For this reason, in-line rifles shooting conicals and jacketed bullets are better choices for long- and short-range shooting. The .50 caliber is really all that is needed to dispatch black bears. Jacketed bullets are available up to 370 grains in that caliber, if not more, and solid lead conicals are available up to 400 grains. So the larger .54 caliber just isn't necessary.

In fact, a .45-caliber conical and jacketed bullet fired from an in-line works nicely on black bears, too, and this caliber is becoming increasingly popular for in-line hunters pursuing deer-sized game and black bears. The smaller caliber and bullet, which offers

These Buckslayer bullets from CVA are typical modern lead conicals for muzzleloaders. They have concave bases to aid expansion, good aerodynamics, and make good choices for bears.

good velocity and a nice trajectory, work because heavy conicals and jacketed bullets are available. Nosler Partition offers a 250-grain saboted .45-caliber bullet, and Power Belt offers its "AroTip" bullet in .45 caliber with 275 grains. Both of these bullets will take black bears out to a hundred yards, perhaps more, and several other manufacturers offer jacketed bullets up to 300 grains in this caliber. Similar weights are also available in solid lead conicals. Buffalo Bullet offers a lead conical with 245 or 285 grains, and the Buckslayer Bullet from CVA is available up to 300 grains.

Try to avoid conical and jacketed bullets that are advertised as having rapid expansion. You want controlled expansion and penetration on black bears, and bullets with rounded or somewhat flattened noses or shallow hollowpoint tips generally do the job better. Some of the so-called "expanding" bullets do work well, though, such as the Expander MX jacketed sabot loads from Barnes and the XTP Mag Sabots from Thompson/Center, both in 300 grain. The Dangerous Game bullet from Power Belt is a great killer, too. It sports a long steel tip that allows good penetration while controlling expansion, even in bone and dense muscle tissue. It's available in 420 and 530 grains in .50 caliber—a bit heavy, but deadly.

For solid lead conicals, the Great Plains bullet from Hornady in 300 grains works extremely well and is one of my favorite loads, as is the 300-grain Buckslayer bullet from CVA and the 385-grain lead conical from Buffalo Bullet.

Regardless of whether you choose a roundball or bullet, make sure to use it with the proper powder charge and know how it performs. Building the ultimate load will take you some time at the range, experimenting with different bullet types and amounts of propellant, but it's crucial to achieving peak performance, especially for black bears. All reproduction sidelock muzzleloaders and in-lines come with an owner's manual that recommends the best loads for various projectiles, as well as maximum powder charges, which should never be exceeded.

As a general rule of thumb, the amount of propellant necessary for big game can be determined by multiplying the caliber by two. So a good charge for a .50-caliber gun would be 100 grains; 108 grains for a .54. The latter number is difficult to achieve consistently with granular powder, so it can be rounded off to 110 grains. However, some guns and projectiles will perform better with slightly more or less powder, so build up or down as needed, making sure to stay within the maximum charge limits from the manufacturer.

The current trend for in-lines seems to be toward heavier powder loads. The word "magnum" has become quite common, and there are a number of in-lines on the market that can accommodate 150 grains of powder, generally in pellet form. It's unfortunate that hunters are accepting this "magnum" name at face value because it's really misleading, and potentially dangerous.

It's a common misconception that more powder means more bullet speed, better trajectories and accuracy, and more power downrange. But this isn't true. To begin with, very few, if any, .50-

This nice bear was taken with a .50-caliber Thompson/Center Hawken Custom, one of the author's favorite replica models.

caliber in-line muzzleloaders built today are capable of fully combusting 150 grains of Pyrodex pellets. This means a portion of the charge is actually wasted during ignition, and the bullet is being propelled by a smaller amount of powder. In fact, 130 volumetric grains of powder is a lot for any in-line to burn completely. Going with larger amounts is a waste of propellant and money.

None of the in-line muzzleloaders I own have shown greater accuracy when charged with more than 120 grains or so of propellant. What you do get is more recoil, more unused powder, worse accuracy and grouping, and quicker barrel wear. Because there is no set standard within the industry to define what a magnum load is, other than a 150-grain charge, and because that charge can be followed by a bullet of any weight, dangerously high pressures can result in some cases.

A sidelock percussion muzzleloader loaded with 90 grains of powder behind a 240- or 250-grain bullet will generally kill a bear

This Knight muzzleloader comes with a synthetic stock complete with a thumb hole and stainless-steel barrel. Loaded with 100 grains of powder and a 300-grain bullet, it easily handled this Newfoundland bruin.

at the right range, and in-line muzzleloaders charged with 110 to 120 grains of powder and larger conical or jacketed bullets will easily do the same. Just don't get carried away or caught up in the magnum craze.

Several different types of propellant can be used with muzzle-loaders these days. Blackpowder is the most traditional, and it's available in granular sizes from Fg up to FFFFg, which is the most common. For black bears, you only have to be familiar with two sizes: FFg and FFFg. FFg works well in .45 caliber and in larger calibers with heavy loads, while FFFg is good with lighter loads. I generally use FFg, but some of my guns do shoot better with FFFg. You'll have to do some testing to find out what works best in your gun.

Blackpowder is an excellent propellant, with a low flash point that works reasonably well in damp or wet conditions. It's also reliable and offers good pressures and velocities once an optimum powder/projectile load has been developed. But it is a bit smelly, with lots of smoke, and it leaves a lot of residue behind. Guns using the stuff should be cleaned regularly.

There are a number of propellant substitutes, or "replicas," on the market, and they are very popular among today's muzzle-loading hunters, especially in-liners. The most common is Pyrodex, from Hodgdon. Its ingredients give it the same basic ballistics and characteristics as blackpowder, and in granular form it's measured volume for volume with blackpowder. A major plus for Pyrodex is that it leaves less residue in the barrel, which means that cleaning is easier and required less often. But Pyrodex does have a higher flash point (it has to get hotter to ignite), so it's not recommended for use in flintlocks. Some hunters claim it is less reliable in wet weather, although in properly cleaned and maintained muzzleloaders this shouldn't be much of a problem. After hunting in rain or snow, I discharge my muzzleloader, swab and wipe it dry, and reload it before heading out the next day.

Pyrodex comes in different granular sizes, and RS, which stands for rifle/shotgun, is the one you'll want for caplocks and in-line muzzleloaders. Pyrodex Select is a more refined and consistent version, and it works extremely well, too.

Pyrodex is also available in pellet form (granular Pyrodex compressed into a snug, compact pill). Pellets are available with 50 grains for .45 caliber, 30 and 50 grains for .50 caliber, and 60 grains for .54 caliber. If you are shooting a .50-caliber in-line and have developed an optimum load that calls for a 100-gain charge, you would simply drop two 50-grain pellets down the barrel. While some traditional shooters feel these pellets are an abomination, many hunters love their convenience and easy loading. It should be noted, however, that while Pyrodex pellets can be used with standard No. 11 or 209 shotgun primers, they aren't recommended for sidelock percussion or flintlock muzzleloaders.

Other substitute propellants include Triple Seven, also from Hodgdon, which is odorless during shooting and cleaning. It is even easier to clean than Pyrodex; plain water is all it takes. It's available in granular form, which can be used with No. 11 or 209 primers, and in pellet form, best used with 209 shotgun primers. Clear Shot is another similar substitute, made by Goex. It comes in several granular sizes and seems to work just as well as the other substitutes, although I've had difficulty finding it in some areas.

Small, handy gadgets like speed loaders and cappers have also made muzzleloaders more convenient, allowing hunters to leave much of the cumbersome traditional equipment at home. Except for a few emergency items like a nipple wrench and nipple pick and extra caps, about the only things I carry are a ball starter and a few pre-loaders and an applicable capper. These fit easily in my pocket or in a small possibles bag attached to my belt.

Quick loaders are plastic tubes that carry a predetermined granular or pellet charge in one end and a projectile in the other. One of the best is the 4-in-1 T-Loader from CVA. It's made of clear heavy-duty plastic, and one end has measurement marks in 10-grain increments highlighted in red, so no separate

Today's blackpowder hunter is able to carry fewer tools afield thanks to cappers and quick loaders. A "possibles" bag like this one is all you need.

measuring device is needed. It will hold up to 110 grains of granular powder or as many as three 50-grain pellets. The other end holds the projectile. The compartment will house some of the heaviest conicals in the .50- and .54-caliber class, even saboted bullets and .490 (.50-caliber) and .530 (54-caliber) roundballs, although patches must be carried separately. Molded into the plastic cap on one end is a place for a No. 11 percussion cap, and there is a small stub on the side that acts as a ball starter. There is also a hole in the side that fits over the end of your ramrod and acts as a T-rod, or "palm saver," as you push the projectile down the barrel to seat it on the charge.

Other quick loaders come in a solid color. They have measurements on the side and are intended to be cut to a specific load. Whatever the case, quick loaders save valuable time when reloading, and limit the amount of paraphernalia that must be carried afield. I never leave the house or camp without them.

Cappers are handy plastic devices designed to hold percussion caps. Most models for sidelock muzzleloaders have a half-dozen or so fingers coming off a center canister, and each finger is designed to hold a single No. 11 percussion cap. The canister itself holds extra caps, too. To cap, or recap, the nipple, simply press one of the caps down onto the nipple and you're ready to go. Because these containers are made of plastic, the caps can be carried and used for loading without a sound.

In-line muzzleloaders require a different type of capper, appropriately called an

This T-loader carries a projectile in one end and propellant in the other. It also acts as a powder measure, ball starter, and T-handle for the ramrod.

"in-line," or "straight-line," capper. The straight, rectangular tube is long and narrow enough to reach into the breech area and seat a cap. These cappers can hold anywhere from nine to fifteen caps, and models are available to accommodate No. 11 percussion caps or 209 shotgun primers.

When you're just starting to develop an optimum load, a powder flask might help, and a standard powder measure will provide slightly more consistent measurements, although I rarely take these items afield anymore. Once I find an optimum load, I put it directly into the quick loader.

An in-line cap remover might be necessary, too. Unlike a sidelock, where the nipple is fully exposed, the nipple on an in-line is harder to reach, making it more difficult to remove caps with your fingers. A cap remover designed specifically for the job is much faster.

I like to use a sling on my muzzleloaders. When hunting behind hounds or on spot-and-stalk hunts, this leaves my hands free and makes long hikes more comfortable. In a treestand, a sling can also be used to hang the rifle from a limb or bow hanger screwed into the tree.

Finally, there is the question of whether to use a scope on a muzzleloader. Be sure to check their legality first, as they aren't allowed everywhere. This restriction usually applies only to special muzzleloader seasons; I'm

Cappers reduce loading time. A straight-line capper (top) is generally used for in-lines, while the "star" type is for sidelocks.

unaware of any state or province that bars them during the general bear season. I don't like scopes on sidelock muzzleloaders, but this is more personal than performance based. Because in-lines reach out farther, scopes make more sense on these guns, and they do help with shot placement.

Something in 1.5X to 2.5X power should be sufficient for most black bear situations, considering range limitations. Muzzle-loaders have considerable recoil and can give a scope quite a jolt, so buy the best scope you can afford, one with good lenses and strong reticles.

While most bear hunting seasons across the continent are governed by fewer restrictions than special deer seasons for muzzle-loaders, a number of states and provinces do have a minimum for caliber or projectile weight. There also may be restrictions on sight systems or ignition systems. Be sure to check. The .45 caliber is not legal for every state or provincial special muzzleloading season, but the .50 caliber is. Except for some of the heavier .45-caliber conicals and sabot loads, the .50 caliber is generally considered the minimum for black bears anyway. And because it's a good caliber for deer and accommodates a variety of projectiles, it's a great all-around choice for big game hunters.

A BRIEF WORD ON SLUG GUNS

Slug guns are becoming increasingly popular for both deer and black bears. Not long ago, about the only slug gun available was a Foster-type, "rifled" slug in a smoothbore barrel, generally Improved Cylinder. These early smoothbore shotguns added little spin for stabilizing slugs, and the maximum range for consistent accuracy was only about fifty yards. Eventually, rifled barrels came along, and though they tossed slugs with a bit more accuracy, it wasn't until recently that things took a dramatic turn for the better.

The biggest improvement came with the introduction of saboted slugs. A plastic sleeve encases the slug and molds into the rifling as it slides down the barrel. This results in a controlled, stabilizing spin on the slug, offering three-inch groups out to 100 yards, perhaps even 125 yards with practice and a scope. For this reason, slug-gun barrels with full rifling the length of the barrel are best.

Because the slug is actually a conical bullet that retains energy downrange, and because the plastic sabot helps maintain pressure within the barrel, today's slugs have impressive velocities. A .45-caliber sabot-encased slug can deliver more than 1,300 foot-pounds of energy out to a hundred yards. Larger .50-caliber slugs in thicker sabots are also available, and their energy is truly impressive.

Still, a slug gun is basically just a rifled shotgun that shoots slugs at less than 2,000 feet per second (at the muzzle). Although far better than the slug guns of yesteryear, they still have a range limitation that any shooter should be careful to stay within. In general, I would compare the slug gun to a modern in-line muzzleloader, with good ballistics on black bears out to 100 to 125 yards.

Chapter
7

HANDGUN HUNTING

I've witnessed many serious debates about which handgun cartridges are best for hunting black bears. And I try hard to stay out of them. As with politics and religion, it seems that every handgun enthusiast has a different opinion. I'm not the most serious handgun hunter, but what I've learned has come the hard way, from actual hunting experience.

Handguns can be deadly on a variety of big game, including black bears. But just like when hunting with a rifle, the right cartridge is critical, so is the type of bullet. Loads from handguns typically travel slower than from rifles, so hunters need as much velocity as possible to reach a bear's vitals through thick fur, dense muscle, and bones. Not muzzle velocity, but impact velocity, where it counts.

To achieve top velocity and range from handgun cartridges, and in most cases the most consistent accuracy as well, longer barrels are a must. Depending on the specific cartridge, guns with four-inch barrels have enough accuracy and power out to forty or fifty yards to bring down a bear. The shot placement is crucial, and for most hunters such accuracy is a stretch. These short-barreled handguns would be sufficient for bait and hound hunting, but for longer shots six-inch barrels are considered the minimum, and seven inches or more adds even more velocity and energy.

Novice handgunners sometimes choose a gun with insufficient power. This means a cartridge that is too small, with a bullet that fails to create a sufficient wound channel or hit the animal with enough energy. Handgunners shooting over bait, in particular, seem to pick bullets that lack proper cohesiveness upon impact; bullets that don't hold together, that shatter and splinter at close range with hot loads.

A handgun cartridge should deliver a bullet with an impact velocity of at least 1,000 feet per second. Again, the key words here are "impact velocity," not muzzle velocity. Very few black bears are shot at the muzzle (thankfully!). Whether you're shooting over bait at twenty yards or out to fifty or sixty yards, the bullet should be traveling 1,000 fps when it hits the bear. While a good

The short-barrel weapon (top) is a good choice for shooting over bait or at bears treed by hounds. For greater distances, stick with a longer barrel.

number of pistol bullets fit this criterion, many lack sufficient power and penetration to get the job done.

Cartridges in .40 caliber or larger diameter are best on black bears. Smaller calibers will certainly kill a black bear under the right conditions, but .40 caliber and larger bullets are usually (but always) faster. They are also heavier, which means more energy transferred downrange. These bullets are available in many shapes and types—hollowpoint, flat-, and snub-nose or softpoint and hard cast, for example. Some work better than others. The .40-caliber bullets open up a larger wound channel, which is always important when hunting black bears. Use a low- to mid-range 200-grain bullet, and you're in business.

Considering the number of handgun cartridges now available, it might be easier to categorize the various loads as those that will kill bear under certain circumstances but aren't really

Black bears can be humanely dispatched with a handgun, but proper caliber selection is important.

hunting cartridges, minimum cartridges for close-range work, and finally the top choices.

Cartridges like the .357 Magnum and .45 ACP will kill bears but aren't really hunting loads. Guns in this group will kill a bear at close range with proper shot placement, but they usually lack the power to be reliable choices for all-around handgun hunting. As of this writing, the 180-grain Partition Gold is the heaviest and hottest load for the .357, and though it is still zipping along at around 1,088 fps at fifty yards, it only packs 473 ft-lbs of energy, which is borderline for killing a black bear even under the best of circumstances. The .357 is also a fairly small bullet that creates a fairly small wound channel. While the hard-cast bullets may go directly through soft tissue at close range, the bear may travel a long distance before dying.

The same is basically true with the .45 ACP and .44 Special. Even when loaded with a 246-grain, round-nose bullet, the .44 S&W Special is only traveling at 725 fps at fifty yards and has just over 300 ft-lbs of energy. In general, the cartridges in this category are just too light and too slow for most black bear hunting situations. Any shots from guns in this category should be well under fifty yards.

Calibers like the .41 magnum and 10mm fall are minimum calibers for close-range work. Both of these are available with 200-grain or larger loads that shoot over 1,000 fps and pack enough power to have a deadly impact on black bears. Based on ballistics, however, they should be limited to under fifty yards, too. At that range, both have enough power to break bone. Loaded with a Winchester 175-grain silvertip hollowpoint, the 10mm zips along at over 1,140 fps at fifty yards and delivers over 500 ft-lbs of energy. The 10mm will also accommodate a full-metal-jacketed, truncated-cone 200-grain bullet. It's a bit slower but packs sufficient punch to kill black bears. Larger bullets are also available.

The .41 magnum is nearly as good. Loaded with a 210-grain jacketed hollowpoint, it sails along at over 1,100 fps at fifty yards and hits with nearly 500 ft-lbs of energy. At twenty-five yards, the results from both the .41 magnum and 10mm are even better, which makes them a good choice for bait and hound hunting, but not much else. Both calibers will accommodate lighter loads, such as the 170 and 180, but these are slower downrange and pack less energy and should be avoided. Stick with the heavier loads.

The best handgun cartridges for black bears are the .44 magnum, .45 magnum, .454. All have speed, hit with a whollop, and, with a partition and jacketed hollowpoint bullet, open up an impressive wound channel. They also have good accuracy and sufficient power beyond the fifty-yard mark. The .44 magnum comes with a 240- or 250-grain bullet. Both are moving at more than a 1,000 fps at fifty yards and pack 600 to 700 ft-lbs of energy, depending upon barrel length.

The .45 magnum is available with a 260-grain bullet. It has plenty of weight, and at fifty yards clips along at more than 1,100 fps and hits the target with 700 ft-lbs of energy. At a hundred yards, the .45 is still traveling at 1,000 fps and hits with more than 600 ft-lbs. It's an effective killer over bait or with hounds, and at shorter spot-and-stalk ranges it'll usually drop a bear on the spot with good shot placement. The .44 and .45 magnums are the most popular calibers among outfitters and guides. For good all-around performance on black bears, they'll serve you well. And they have good accuracy and manageable recoil.

The .454 is the granddaddy of the group. This is a real bear killer, with near rifle-like ballistics. Cartridges are commonly available in 260- and 300-grain, and at fifty yards both are cruising at more than 1,400 fps and have over 1,400 ft-lbs of energy. This cartridge will stop any black bear on the continent, but given its weight and heavy recoil it may not be the right choice for everyone.

Of course, the above discussion doesn't include any of the wildcat and big-bore calibers now available, such as the .480 Ruger, .450 Marlin, and 45/70. All are good bear killers, as long as you don't mind the added recoil. And let's not forget the Contender and Encore from Thompson/Center. Both are designed to accommodate some of the most familiar and powerful cartridges in the world, with rifle-like velocity, power, and accuracy.

The Contender is currently available in 12-, 14-, and 16-inch barrels and in cartridges like the .44 Remington Magnum, 45/70, even the .30–30. The newer Encore comes with either a 12- or 15-inch barrel and has even more caliber options, including the .454 Casull, .480 Ruger, .308 Winchester, .30–06 Springfield, and .450 Marlin. It even comes in a .50-caliber magnum muzzleloading pistol that takes a 209 shotgun primer. Remember that faster velocities and more energy will be obtained from the longer barrels in each model. These are both single-shot hand-

The Contender (top) and Encore from Thompson/Center are popular among black bear hunters. Both are available in a wide range of calibers and can be equipped with scopes.

guns, but with the right cartridge and proper shot placement one shot will be all you need for black bears.

As with caliber selection, the best bullet is also a hot topic among black bear enthusiasts. Some prefer hard-cast bullets, while others swear by softer bullets or hollowpoints. They all work, and there are valid arguments in support of each.

The hard-cast bullets offer great penetration and bust bone better than anything else. In front of hot cartridges, however, the larger and heavier bullets in this class have a tendency to pass right through hair, skin, fat, and soft tissue, leaving small wound channels. The bear will die, but there may be little blood, which makes for tough tracking. My experience with hard-cast bullets has shown that it's best to hit bone first, ideally the front shoulder, in the hope that the bullet and shattered bone fragments will continue into the lung/heart area with good integrity and enough energy to do some damage.

While some guides and outfitters I've hunted with over the years disagree, I see nothing wrong with hollowpoints for hand-guns on black bears. At handgun velocities, particularly when driven as fast as possible from a six-inch or longer barrel, a 240- to 260-grain hollowpoint works very well. It's true that they don't break bone as well as hard-cast bullets, or penetrate as deeply, but in soft tissue like the lungs they really don't have to. Hollowpoints still do a respectable job on bone, often shattering it and sending pieces of lead and bone fragments into the vitals. They also create more shock and tissue damage, which causes more bleeding. And more times than not, a second shot is possible while the bear remains in shock from the initial hit.

I would only recommend hollowpoints in .44 magnum or larger cartridges, however, due to available bullet weight, impact speed, and energy downrange. But I think they are a better choice for black bears than hard-cast bullets.

Many experienced hunters, guides, and outfitters prefer softer, flat-nosed cartridges. I like them, too. They maintain speed and energy, offer good penetration and expansion, and transfer speed and energy into the target with good integrity, while opening a respectable wound channel. They also work well on bone and soft tissue.

Using handguns for black bears is a lot of fun, but as with any weapon, it's important to understand their capabilities and limitations before heading into the woods. Some states have minimum caliber requirements for big game, so be sure to check the regulations in the area you plan to hunt, or check with your guide or outfitter. Incidentally, don't hesitate to ask for caliber and cartridge recommendations when booking a guided hunt.

Finally, while handguns are legal for hunting in the United States, non-residents are not allowed to carry handguns into Canada.

Chapter

8

THE BEAR SEASONS

Spring! The word tantalizes the tongue like an ice-cold beer during the dog days of summer. Despite being born and raised in Maine, where long, harsh winters are the norm, I've never particularly enjoyed the cold season. After a fresh snow, I might take an occasional walk to see what has been moving in the woods surrounding the house, and once in a while the wife might get me out for some cross-country skiing, but once the fall hunting season ends and winter sets in I go into hibernation, rarely emerging until spring except to plow the driveway or keep the wood stove fed. The calendar says that spring arrives on March 20, but in my neck of the woods it rarely comes until April or May.

After all that time indoors, I'm usually itching to get outside. With its miracle of new life and rebirth, spring rejuvenates my heart and soul. But there is another reason I look forward to spring—black bear season.

At one time, spring hunting seasons were quite common in the United States, but they are becoming increasingly rare these days. Although some closures are based on solid science, in most cases doing away with spring hunting has little to do with black bear populations. In fact, numbers are stable or increasing in most states. Most such closures have been the result of changing public opinion about when and how black bears should be hunted, and well-financed animal rights and anti-hunting groups have often been involved.

Although attempts to close the spring season failed in Idaho and Michigan in 1996, Colorado voters did away with their spring hunt in 1992. The main concern among those opposed to spring hunting is the killing of sows with cubs, even though this practice is prohibited in nearly every state.

Of the twenty-eight states that currently allow black bear hunting, only seven still have a spring season: Alaska, Arizona, Idaho, Montana, Oregon, Washington (not really a spring season, but their fall season begins in mid-July), and Wyoming. Despite the fact that some eastern states like Maine and Michigan have populations equal to or greater than many states west of the Mississippi River, all the states with a spring season are located in

the West. Most spring seasons take place sometime from April through June. Because changes to seasons or regulations can occur at any time, always check with the appropriate wildlife agency for current information.

All twenty-eight states that now allow black bear hunting have fall seasons.

This bear was taken back when Maine still had a spring season. Most states now have bear hunting seasons in the fall only.

Most of these take place sometime from August through November, with season lengths varying from just three days in Pennsylvania to year-round in some areas of Alaska. Nationwide, the average fall hunting season runs about two weeks. Because specific season dates vary greatly from state to state and are apt to change from year to year due to population trends and other factors, hunters should always contact the appropriate wildlife agency to get an update on current season dates and regulations.

North of the border in Canada, things are a whole lot different. Black bears can be hunted in every province and territory during the fall (except on Prince Edward Island, which has no bears), and only two provinces don't allow spring bear hunting. One is Ontario, which closed its spring season in 1999 based on popular opinion rather than bear populations. This province has a large bear population, and efforts are underway to reinstate the spring season. The other province with no spring season is Nova Scotia,

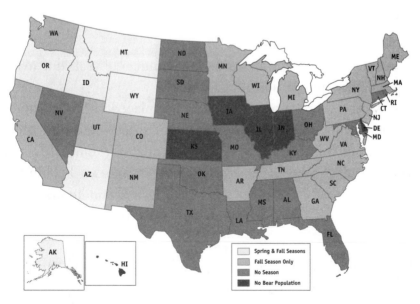

Black bear hunting seasons, United States.

▢	Spring & Fall Seasons
▨	Fall Season Only
■	No Bear Population

Yukon Territory

Northwest Territories

British Columbia

Alberta

Manitoba

Saskatchewan

Ontario

Quebec

Newfoundland

Prince Edward Island

New Brunswick

Nova Scotia

Black Bear Hunting Seasons, Canada

which hasn't had a spring season for a number of years due to an unstable bear population.

Most spring seasons in Canada take place in May and June, although some start as early as April and extend into July. Most fall seasons occur from late August through November. In the Yukon and Northwest Territories, black bears can be hunted nearly year-round under certain guidelines and conditions.

SPRING

I often get asked whether spring or fall is more productive for black bear hunting. My initial instinct is to say, "Spring," because this is my favorite time to hunt. But the truth is that both seasons offer prime opportunities to hunt this animal. The best chances of seeing bears and obtaining a trophy in terms of pelt condition and size is really a matter of weather conditions and timing.

Still, if I were forced to pick one season over the other, it would be spring. Black bears generally emerge from their winter dens sometime in April or May, during the early stages of green-up. And they are still wearing their winter coats. The underfur is thick and wool-like and the guard hairs long and full. Except for late fall and during hibernation, the overall pelt will never be in better condition. But it doesn't last forever.

In most areas, pelt condition is generally good from April through much of June. As spring temperatures start to warm, the fur starts to shed and show signs of thinning. Some black bears may also accelerate the shedding by rubbing against trees, further degrading the pelt. So in general terms, the later the spring hunt, the less likely you'll find a perfect pelt.

When this thinning actually occurs, however, depends on the region and prevailing weather conditions. In the high mountains of northern Idaho or western Wyoming, for example, spring comes late, and black bears may not emerge from their dens until May. Getting into that high country can be difficult, if not impossible, that early due to the lingering snowpack, but if you do, rubbing and thinning might not be noticeable on most bears until late June. I have observed black bears in northern Labrador in July with coats as thick as wool.

In New Brunswick, southern Quebec, and across the southernmost portion of the other provinces signs of rubbing and thinning might be noticeable as early as the end of May or in early June.

The earlier and warmer the spring, the faster pelt conditions deteriorate. Of course, there are always exceptions. An early spring in the far north or high country might see bears emerge

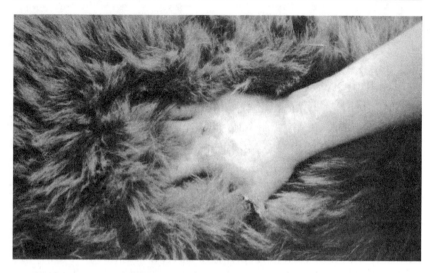

Black bears are covered with thick underfur in early spring, which they shed by late spring and regrow in the fall.

These bears were taken in late May in western Canada, and their pelts are still in excellent condition.

earlier than normal, and thinning will therefore occur earlier, as well. A late spring, even in warmer climates, or a cold snap might delay things a week or two.

I've taken bears the last week of June that were still in pretty good shape, at least when viewed from a distance. Up close, however, it wasn't unusual for the thick underfur to be thin or all but gone. The longer guard hairs were likely to be thin, as well, especially along the underbelly and where the chest meets the front legs. The second or third week of June is more or less the cut-off date for killing black bears in prime condition in most areas. After that, the hunter may have to pick and choose.

Without doubt, a pelt is in the best condition when a black bear emerges from its winter den, although this isn't necessarily when you're most likely to spot a bear. A certain percentage of bears will be out and about as early as April, and most will be up and moving by early May. Males generally emerge from the dens first, but it's not until mid- or late May that they start covering a lot of territory in search of females interested in breeding. All the females will probably have emerged by then, too, and while you might see more sows while scouting or sitting over bait, chances are better that you'll see more males because of their extensive roaming in

This large boar was taken during the spring season. It was traveling with a sow, which is not uncommon during the breeding period.

search of receptive females. This interest in breeding typically continues through much of June.

So the best time to see lots of black bears and hunt for quality pelts is from early or mid-May into the middle of June. The latter part of June can be good, too, especially in the north and in higher elevations, but signs of thinning will start showing up.

Another reason these weeks are tops for spring bears is that weather conditions have generally settled down by then. The winds are calmer, snow and cold snaps are less likely except in the far north and high elevations, and rain is more predictable. Extreme temperature variations are also less likely. In fact, during May, even early June in the north, daytime temperatures are still cool or gradually warming, both of which lead to peak bear activity. Sudden cold fronts, snow squalls with sudden temperature changes, periods of heavy rain, hot temperatures, and high winds make hunting difficult. Bears will move under these conditions, but they seem to do so less often.

A drizzle with light winds, or before and after a sudden spring shower, can be great, though. Black bears will continue to feed and remain highly active, but there's often little wind, and human scent is difficult to detect. In hard-hunted areas, such conditions may mean fewer hunters in the field. Bears seem to sense this, and their activity level may rise. Also, when the ground is wet, bears can move through the woods with less sound, and as daytime temperatures rise, a slow rain helps keep them cool. Their heavy coats of underfur and guard hair shed water easily, so a drizzle is of no consequence to them, and they may move around at any hour of the day.

This is true in the fall when bears are on a feeding binge, but especially so in the spring when the breeding season is on. So while other hunters stay in camp and play cards while waiting for better weather, it pays to spend extra time on the stand or glassing the slopes.

But when really nasty weather hits, those bears will hold tight somewhere until it breaks. You should try to be in the woods when it does, because bear activity will definitely increase, especially after a day or two.

Ideal spring weather has gradually warming temperatures and consistent, stable weather patterns with light to medium winds or no wind at all. The best chance for this usually comes from the middle of May through the middle of June.

Blackflies, mosquitoes, and other biting insects haven't reached their peak in May, which makes sitting on a treestand or walking in the woods a while lot easier and more enjoyable. They can be a bother starting in mid- to late May or early June in Canada's bear country and in Alaska, sometimes earlier depending on spring conditions or local habitat. Biting insects are less of a problem in much of the Western high country, which is one reason I enjoy hunting there so much. But to play it safe, even in the West, I always go prepared with fly dope, a head net, and gloves—spring or fall.

Spring-killed black bear generally makes better table fare. I even prefer it to most types of venison. Although there is absolutely nothing wrong with bear meat taken in the fall, bears lose so much fat and weight during the winter that their meat is

Depending on the temperature, bugs can be a problem by late spring. This small bear was taken in New Brunswick.

much leaner and therefore better eating. Some hunters persist in believing that spring bears aren't good to eat, largely because bears feast on winter-killed game at this time of year. But they'll eat carrion anytime they come across it, spring, summer, or fall, so this theory doesn't hold water. Most of the bear's spring diet actually consists of grasses and other vegetation, which they find on south-facing slopes and along waterways.

If there is anything negative about the spring season, it's that adult bears weigh less than they do in the fall. It's not unusual for bruins to lose 20 or 30 percent of their weight while in their winter den. So a 300-pounder in the fall might weigh just 210 pounds or so in the spring. This weight loss generally has little effect on skull size, but if you like to measure your bears in terms of total weight, the spring isn't the best time to do it.

The heaviest and biggest bears are almost always taken in the fall. In fact, unless the bear is an old boar or sow that has already maximized growth potential, it will have added even more weight by fall than it lost over the previous winter. The skull will also be slightly larger in the fall. The skull doesn't shrink with winter weight loss, but it continues to get larger as the animal matures.

FALL

The same concerns about pelt condition that affect hunters late in the spring season are also a problem for hunters when the season opens in the fall. Many fall hunting seasons commence in late August or early September, and while the chances of seeing lots of bears at that time are good, pelt condition is often poor, except perhaps in far northern areas. Black bears are still in their summer coats or just beginning to grow their winter covering, but in either case, pelts are less than prime.

It's usually the middle of September before pelts are in reasonably good shape in most regions, and it might be late September or well into October before the underfur and guard hairs are fully grown on a prime pelt. Where black bears are still out and about in November, which is just about everywhere except the far north, pelts are even better. In general, the closer you get to hibernation the better the coat will be.

Another problem with hunting very early in the season is the potential for hot weather. I have hunted more than once in Maine and the Maritime provinces of Canada, even in the higher elevations of the West, in temperatures into the seventies, and such weather has definitely slowed down bear activity. Bears tend to concentrate movements very early or late in the day, often after dark when temperatures are coolest. Your productive hunting time is reduced, and your chance of success along with it, especially for the biggest black bears, which are most bothered by the heat.

There is also the problem of flies. They are usually less of an issue in the fall, but on warm days in late August through the middle of September, they can be as numerous and bothersome as they are in June. Hunters should be prepared with fly dope,

This bear was killed in early September in northern Quebec. In the far north, black bears may offer prime pelts very early in the fall season.

head nets and gloves, and should make a point to deal with any harvested bears quickly.

This isn't to say that you should avoid hunting in late August and early September. This can actually be a very productive time, especially the first week or so of the season, when bears are off guard and not expecting human contact. But as this is a transition period between summer and fall, the weather patterns may fluctuate between wet and dry, warm and cool, even hot and cold, all of which can throw off a bear's schedule.

Optimum conditions for bear activity at this time of year are much the same as mid-May to mid-June: consistently cool weather patterns, perhaps mixed with light rain, or a gradual decline in temperatures, ideally with little or no wind. These weather conditions are most prevalent across black bear range during the last two weeks of September and the first two weeks of October. My experience in the fall as been that this is the best period to hunt in most areas, with the possible exception of the first week of the season.

There are other advantages to targeting these weeks, as well. Many of the wild berry crops will have ripened and been eaten already, so bears will be looking for food elsewhere, and bait sites will have a little less competition. Look for bears around any remaining berry patches, agricultural fields, and orchards. If these food sources are gone, they will be into acorns, beechnuts, and other hard mast.

Big boars like this one are usually solitary in the fall, but in spring they'll cover lots of territory looking for females to breed with.

Black bears are well into their feeding frenzy at this time of year, trying to put on as much weight as possible before taking to the dens. They will be out and about for longer periods of time and covering a lot of territory, which greatly increases your chances of seeing them. Just like you would during the mid-May to mid-June period, plan to spend more times in the woods from mid-September through mid-October.

There are also less hunters in the woods at this time. Most fall bear hunters are eager to hit the woods early in the season. This is usually true even in states and provinces that also offer spring hunting. Where baiting is legal, hunting later can be advantageous because bears that were hitting bait sites that have been discontinued for the season will be looking elsewhere. So bait sites that were being hit by one or two bears early in the season may be visited by several more bears later on.

Those old bait sites are also good places to start tracking with hounds, since bears accustomed to feeding there will continue to check in from time to time. These sites remain ripe with scent until cold weather or rain washes it away.

While boars normally emerge from the dens earlier than sows in the spring, most also remain active longer in the fall, so your chances of taking a male increase as the fall season progresses.

So some weeks are definitely better for hunting than others in both spring and fall, depending on a wide variety of factors, but there's no need to get too scientific or specific. Bears are still unpredictable much of the time. If you get a chance to hunt, get out there and do it. Most of the pleasure of hunting lies in establishing baits and stands and working the dogs, in scouting and glassing beautiful country. Just as with other big game, once the trigger is pulled or the arrow flies, it's all work.

Chapter

9

PLANNING A HUNT

I love bear camps. It makes little difference whether this means a set of tents clustered in the wilderness or a fancy lodge with wall-to-wall carpeting and a hot tub outside the door. If it's in bear country, really good bear country, then it's fine with me.

While the number of hunters baiting, running hounds, and spot-and-stalk hunting on their own has increased over the years, a good many novice bear hunters quickly give up on the idea and opt for the services of a guide or outfitter the next time around. Probably 80 percent of all the black bears harvested across North America each year are taken with the help of a professional. When you stop to think about it, the reasons for this are quite obvious.

Establishing productive bait sites involves a great deal of time and effort. You may decide to start such sites on a part-time basis on weekends a few weeks before the season opens, but once the sites become active during the season these baits need to be checked daily, ideally on a regular schedule. Properly maintaining these baits suddenly takes on a whole new perspective, and with all the other commitments associated with everyday life, not everyone has the time. That initial enthusiasm wears off quickly. For most hunters, this means leaving it to the pros.

Outfitters often take you into country you might not be able to reach on your own.

And running your own bait sites isn't always cheap. Unless you have free access to the great amount and variety of bait needed to attract and keep bears active, the dollars add up quickly. Plus, it has to be retrieved, stored, and transported to the site. All of this can easily total several hundred dollars for just a few days to perhaps two weeks of hunting.

Even if bait is readily available and free, baiting bears represents a serious investment. One outfitter I hunt with regularly recently told me it costs him a minimum of $250 to establish and maintain each bait site he uses during the fall hunting season. He operates in Maine on private land owned by a large paper company, and therefore must pay bait-station permit fees, but self-baiters may end up spending hundreds of dollars dealing with all the various aspects of baiting, too. And unless you hunt your own property or have access to hunting lands nearby, you may have to spend an hour or two driving to and baiting each stand—daily.

But first you have to find a place to hunt. A good many hunters now reside in suburbia, or in areas far from prime bear country. In most cases, the land we hunt is private, which means permission or permits must be obtained, and not all landowners— even those who allow hunting on their land—are open to the idea of having baits on their property. If baiting is allowed on state

Careful planning can result in a good-sized bear such as this one. Hunter Peter Fiduccia took this 200-pounder near Jackman, Maine, with his .30–06.

or federal land in your area, there is often an extraordinary list of rules and regulations to follow.

After you consider all of the above, booking a quality bait hunt with an outfitter or guide starts to look more appealing. They'll do all the work and worrying for an affordable price that generally includes the baiting and active stands, meals, guides, lodging, and game care. Compared to other types of big game hunts, bait hunts for black bears with a reputable outfitter can be one of the best deals going.

Hound hunts typically cost more than bait hunts due to the expense of maintaining and training the hounds, and the risk of their injury or death, but they are worth the investment. Few hunters these days have the time and resources to manage a pack of hounds year-round. Without outfitters, most hunters would never get to experience this exciting and traditional method of hunting.

Probably the easiest and least expensive way to hunt black bears on your own is by using spot-and-stalk techniques near natural food areas. However, this means that you have to live close enough to bear country to be able to scout for good territory before the season. And then you have to worry about whether those foods will be available when the time comes to hunt. As every hunter knows, there are years with bumper crops of hard and soft

You can hunt black bears on your own by setting up a basic camp, but it takes a lot of dedication.

mast, and years when they are scarce. This can have a drastic effect on where you should be hunting.

CHOOSING A GUIDE OR OUTFITTER

As much as I like doing my own thing, most of my bear hunts over the years have been with guides and outfitters. Using their services, and relying on their expertise, simply makes things a whole lot easier—and more productive. Fortunately, quality guides and outfitters specializing in bear hunting are readily available in nearly every state and province that offers a bear season. You'll find their advertisements in various hunting magazines, and many of them have exhibits at the growing number of outdoor shows and expos each winter. Others can be found by contacting state or provincial wildlife departments, guide and outfitter associations, booking agents, and member services of organizations like the North American Hunting Club. (A list of these publications, agencies, and associations can be found in the appendix.)

Arranging a guided black bear hunt is no more different than booking a hunt for any other big game animal. Deciding where to hunt and booking early are among the most important aspects. Considering all the great places to hunt this animal, and the number of guides and outfitters available, deciding where to hunt might take some time.

Once you know how and when you want to hunt, the task gets much easier. For example, some outfitters and guides specialize in only bait or hound hunts, sometimes both, while others are spot-and-stalk only. Whether a state allows baiting or hounds will narrow the field, and only a few Western states continue to offer spring bear hunts. If you're interested in taking a color-phase bear, you should consider an outfitter in the West, perhaps in Manitoba or Alberta, northern Idaho, parts of Colorado, or the Southwest. If you want to hunt with a handgun, Canada is off limits.

Do you want the option of taking a second bear? Few places in the East offer that opportunity. How far are you willing to travel? Flying opens up all of North America, and even with heightened terrorist alerts and tightened security at airports traveling with firearms and archery equipment poses little problem. Do you want a remote pack-in trip by horse or mule? A wilderness fly-in trip by floatplane? Do you want a tent camp or lodge? Pick the brains of friends and acquaintances who have hunted bear in a particular area or with a particular outfitter to get ideas or recommendations.

Next, it's time to contact a few guides or outfitters. I like to call them so I can talk directly to whoever is in charge. Tell them what you're looking for in a hunt and how you plan to hunt—bow, rifle, handgun, or muzzleloader. Let them know how many

Tent camps, like this one in western Wyoming, make it possible to hunt remote areas.

hunters will be in your party and make sure they can accommodate that number. A phone call also offers an opportunity to gain a rapport with the outfitter, to get a feel for the person on the other end of the phone. You can tell a great deal by the way a guide or outfitter talks to you and answers your questions, so listen carefully and read between the lines. I like a guide who speaks with knowledge and enthusiasm.

You might also ask about success rates. Any guide or outfitter posting a harvest rate of 50 percent or better is doing well. Go over exactly how you'd like to hunt and make them aware of any health problems or special needs. If you like what you hear, ask for some brochures and other material on their operation, perhaps a video if they have one, and find out if they have a website, which can be much more informative than printed material. Most websites have pictures of bear taken and the accommodations, perhaps even of some of the country you will be hunting, and other helpful information.

Make contact with the references they offer. Not all of them, but at least a half dozen or so. How did their hunt go? Was the guide or outfitter professional? Did they see bears? If so, how many and what size? If they were hunting with bows over bait, were the stands properly set up for bowhunting? How were the accommodations, the food? Did the outfitter deliver on services promised? Were the animals properly caped, cared for in camp, and prepared for shipment home? And perhaps most importantly, would they hunt with the outfitter again? Keep in mind, though, that any references provided by the outfitter are likely to be good, so don't rely on them exclusively.

Contact the state or provincial fish and wildlife department and any outfitter associations. Are there any complaints from clients or violations against the outfitter? Are they insured, bonded, or licensed to operate? Not all states and provinces require guides and outfitters to be bonded, but they usually must be insured, and all states and provinces require guides and outfitters to be licensed to operate. Being bonded adds some degree of assurance that the outfitter or guide will deliver on services promised since he can be held financially responsible.

When you have the right outfitter or guide for your hunt, then you can get down to details. Place another phone call. Make sure you understand what the total cost is and specifically what is and isn't included in the price. Most outfitter black bear hunts these days are operated on the American-type plan, which includes meals, lodging, guide service, maintained baits and stands on bait hunts, skinning and tending of your bear in camp and getting it ready for shipment home, perhaps even pickup and dropoff at the airport. Find out everything you can. For example, will you need a sleeping bag, or towels? Sometimes you do, sometimes you don't. What is the weather typically like? What should you bring for clothing?

Licenses and tags are generally extra, but not always, so be sure to ask. If you'll be flying into a remote camp by floatplane, is that cost included? Tips to the guides and cook are always extra, too. Tips are a touchy subject, but if the guide does his job well 10 to 12 percent of the cost of hunt is not an unreasonable amount. If the guide really goes above and beyond the line of duty, a larger tip might be called for. Keep in mind that guides can't control the weather and how much game will be seen, so even if you are unsuccessful, tipping a knowledgeable, hard-working guide is a good idea.

The same is true of camp cooks. They work just as hard as the guides, if not harder, although their tips are generally smaller. I usually hunt with a partner or in a group, and each of us typically puts in a contribution of $25 to $100, depending on the size of the party. Tips are discretionary, but remember that some guides working for an outfitter aren't paid a large base salary each week, and tips can make all the difference.

Guided hunts generally vary from outfitted hunts. Outfitters do just what it sounds like, they "outfit" the entire hunt and supply everything needed once in camp, while guided hunts may be more basic. In some cases, clients hiring only a guide are responsible for supplying their own food, doing their own cooking, arranging accommodations, and taking care of their own game, among other things. Some guide services may have a set of rustic camps or cottages for rent close to where you'll hunt, although these may not be included in the basic cost of the hunt, so be sure to check. I have even been on bait hunts where an operation supplied meals, lodging, stands and bait, but the hunter did his own baiting.

Whatever the case, it's imperative to know prior to booking, and especially before sending a deposit, exactly what you are buying. If possible, get it in writing. When you submit a deposit, make sure to get a receipt showing the total cost, deposit, balance due, and due date.

Fully outfitted black bear hunts—not including licenses and tags, personal items, or any lodging required in town before or after the hunt—can run anywhere from $1,300 to more than $2,000, perhaps more. Prices are generally quoted in U.S. funds, even in Canada. On fully outfitted hunts, deposits run a quarter to a third of the price of the hunt per person, with the balance paid thirty to sixty days prior to the hunt. Some outfitters allow the final payment upon arrival.

Hiring just a guide and not much else should run much less, but by the time you add up lodging, meals, and everything else, you might not be saving a whole lot. For inexperienced bear hunters, or hunters traveling to an area for the first time, a hunt with an outfitter is the best way to go because just about everything is taken care of. All the hunter has to do is hunt.

Make sure you understand the cancellation policy, too. Some deposits are non-refundable; the deposit will be held for a future hunt or will be returned with sufficient notice, generally sixty to ninety days prior to hunt. Don't forget to ask about how to obtain licenses and tags.

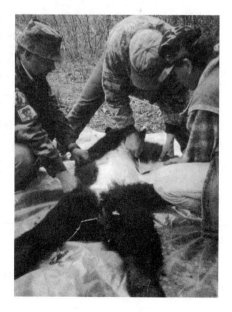

On outfitted hunts, the guides are usually responsible for skinning.

They might be available directly from the outfitter or guide in camp, or they may have to be purchased in a local town prior to heading into the bush. Some outfitters will purchase them prior to your arrival and have them waiting for you. If this is the case, it's not unusual for the outfitter or guide to ask for the price of the license or tags in advance, usually thirty days or so before the hunt. This will be in addition to the deposit.

If you'll be hunting with muzzleloaders after flying to your destination using a commercial airline, this is also a good time to check on the availability of propellant. Is it available locally and will you have time to purchase what you need before heading into camp? If not, inform the outfitter or guide specifically what you want and ask if he can purchase it for you in advance.

It sounds like there's a lot to this process, but it really isn't that difficult. Having been through it literally hundreds of times over the years, I now know automatically what to ask and how things work, whether it be a black bear hunt or any big game adventure. If you've been on hunts for moose, elk, caribou, deer, and other

In many areas, outfitters use ATVs to reach prime bear country.

game with an outfitter or guide, the procedure is roughly the same. If you're a first-timer, just remember that there are no stupid questions. Ask about everything, no matter how mundane.

Selecting a guide or outfitter and confirming dates for a hunt should be done at least six months in advance, because the best hunting weeks generally fill up first. Top outfitters are often booked a year in advance.

If you're planning a bear hunt to Canada, keep in mind that all firearms must now be registered with Canada Customs prior to entering the country. It's also important to declare all firearms (including bows) with U.S. Customs prior to leaving the United States. This declaration merely serves as proof of ownership prior to entering Canada. The declaration with U.S. Customs can be done at most U.S. airports or at the border.

Hunters entering Canada will be required to fill out a Non-Resident Firearm Declaration, Form JUS 909. These forms are available from the Canada Firearms Center by telephoning 1-800-731-4000, or may be downloaded online at www.cfc.gc.ca. Every hunter must fill out one of these forms, and to save time at the border it's recommended that these forms are filled out in advance, in triplicate. *But leave the signature block empty, because the form must be signed at the border in the presence of a Canadian Customs officer.* Some form of photo identification will be required. The cost of declaration is $50 (Canadian), and it's valid for up to sixty days.

Hunters will only have to pay the $50 once within a twelve-month period, though. In other words, if you travel to Canada for a spring black bear hunt, the same declaration can be used on a fall hunt, providing the same firearm is used. A different firearm can be added to the declaration, however. Bows don't have to be declared under the Canada Firearms Law, but as mentioned above, it's still a good idea to declare them with U.S. Customs prior to entering Canada.

BEAR CAMP

Bear camps can vary from simple to sublime, but on fully outfitted hunts there are basically two types: tents camps and permanent camps or lodges. In my experience, the type of sleeping and eating arrangements has very little to do with the quality of the hunt or the quality of game the hunter can expect to encounter.

I thoroughly enjoy being in a tent camp and hunting wilderness areas that are only accessible by floatplane or packhorse, more for the overall experience than just the hunting. But simply hunting from such a camp is no guarantee of killing trophy black bear or even of seeing more bears than at lodges closer to civilization. Many factors affect how a hunt will go. In theory, bears in remote areas will be less educated to hunting pressure and therefore might come to baits more readily or move more freely. But in reality, I have seen and taken just as many respectable black bears in areas closer to human development, even in areas that receive solid hunting pressure.

Still, if I had to give an edge to one or the other, it would be tent camps, primarily because they are mobile and can be relocated if bears in a certain area are over-hunted, and size begins to diminish. Outfitters who use permanent lodges combat this by carefully managing the areas they hunt, rotating or resting them from year to year. And for the most part, the quality of the hunt is pretty close to even.

The big difference between camps and lodges obviously lies in convenience and amenities. Tent camps are usually basic, although most have wooden floors to keep everything off the ground. Cots or bunk beds and wood stoves are the general rule, as is a separate mess tent where meals are served. There will be bathroom facilities, although this sometimes means an outhouse, and most camps have some type of shower, perhaps just a "sun shower" (basically just a plastic bag that dispenses hot water). Successful tent camps, those in business for a long time, are usually warm and dry and relatively comfortable. Some even have generators for electricity.

Lodges and permanent camps generally offer more comforts. I have hunted from a few that go as far as providing maid service, wall-to-wall carpeting, satellite television, a sauna, and private bathroom, but that is top of the line. Most are much simpler: separate cabins or bedrooms in the lodge, bathroom facilities with showers, kitchen, dining and gathering area, and sometimes electricity. These days, there's a lodge or camp out there that matches the taste of virtually every hunter; just check your outfitter's literature or website to make sure his set-up is what you're looking for.

The type of camp and its location will dictate how much gear you can bring. If you're driving, you can probably haul in

Most tent camps offer plenty of warmth and comfort.

This camp in Quebec offers full bathroom facilities, showers, and private sleeping cabins.

anything you want, but floatplanes, boats, and packhorses mean only essential items will fit. Most outfitters on these types of hunts will set a weight limit for each hunter's gear. Airlines are also becoming increasing stringent on the number of bags that can be checked with each passenger without paying an additional fee. And with a $50 to $75 charge for each additional bag, it pays to leave unnecessary items at home.

After years of packing for a wide variety of bear camps in different settings, my personal list of baggage has pretty much become standardized. It includes the following:

- sleeping bag, if required
- rifle, ammunition, cleaning kit, and/or bow or related hunting equipment
- toilet kit that includes toothbrush, toothpaste, floss, deodorant or antiperspirant, soap, towel/washcloth, small bottle of shampoo, personal medications, aspirin, Aleve or ibuprofen, Pepto-Bismol, insect repellant, lip balm, Neosporin,

Hunters traveling to a remote camp by floatplane should be aware of weight limits for gear.

calamine lotion and/or Cortaid, glasses, contacts and cleaning solution, fingernail clippers, small sewing kit
• boots and camp moccasins
• two extra shirts for camp and hunting
• two extra pairs of pants for camp and hunting
• clean set of clothes for traveling home
• four or five pairs of socks
• camouflage hunting clothes
• sunglasses
• light to medium jacket and vest; heavy jacket if hunting early or late in the year
• rain gear
• binoculars or spotting scope
• knife(s) and sharpening stone
• flashlight and extra batteries
• hat and gloves
• compass/GPS
• small canteen or water bottle

- small tape measure
- cheesecloth
- camera and film
- reading material
- surveyor's tape
- a length of rope
- pen and small pad of paper
- small fannypack or backpack
- snacks (candy bars, granola, etc.)
- fishing gear, if applicable

Depending on the type of hunt you book, a typical day in bear camp may vary. Spot-and-stalk hunters and hunters using hounds generally have the longest days afield and put in the most work filling their tags. Both require long hikes each day, often through rugged country. Although the actual schedule will depend on the outfitter and current conditions, the average hunt starts before sunrise or just after breakfast in order to take advantage of fresh scent left during the night or during early-morning feeding activity. And it can last until well after dark.

I have been on two hound hunts and one spot-and-stalk hunt where circumstances dictated spending the night in the bush. On two other occasions, the guide opted to stay afield while the hunters were sent back to camp. Anything can happen, no matter how well planned the hunt is.

Carry an ample supply of water and snacks such as candy or energy bars. I also bring an extra pair of socks, a compass or GPS, binoculars or spotting scope, and rain gear in a daypack. Just in case, I also carry a small emergency kit with instant coffee, soup mix, matches, collapsible tin cup, and a survival blanket. The entire kit is stowed in a plastic Ziploc bag in my pack and hardly weighs a

When hunters reach camp they should take a few minutes to make sure their rifles are still properly sighted in.

thing. I've been teased about it a time or two over the years, but it sure comes in handy on nights when I'm caught out in the bush.

One of the biggest reasons hunters fail to fill tags on spot-and-stalk and hound hunts is that they aren't physically prepared for the challenge. It always surprises me when hunters spend whatever is necessary to acquire the best clothing, footgear, and other hunting equipment, yet put so little investment in their own bodies.

While I was hunting in northern Idaho a couple of years ago, a hunter arrived in camp during the middle of the week for a hound hunt. He was young, perhaps in his mid-thirties, and looked to be in decent shape. Over coffee the first morning of his hunt he was asked several times if he was ready for the rigorous days ahead. All the other hunters in camp were hunting over bait, including me.

The young hunter proclaimed, perhaps a bit boastfully, that he was a former Special Forces soldier and didn't foresee any problem keeping up. To make a long story short, when he sat down for our late night snack that evening he looked completely worn out. He nearly fell asleep in his soup. He bagged his bear the next day, but was much more humble about his stamina—in fact, he stayed in camp to sleep the next two days.

Get yourself in shape before a bear hunting trip. If you're going to spend the time and money to make it happen, don't ruin your trip—and maybe your health—by neglecting this element. Even if you're in tip-top physical condition, you'll hit the hay exhausted each night, and the next day will start just as early.

Bait hunters have it a bit easier. Depending on the area being hunted, stands over bait may be at least partly accessible by truck, boat, or horse, although there's almost always some walking involved. And getting to some remote stands can be quite a chore. Sitting motionless in a stand for four to six hours each day can be physically challenging, as well. By the time you climb down and head out, there's a good chance you'll feel muscles you never thought you had.

On most commercial bait hunts, hunters head for the stands sometime after lunch. Guides use the morning hours for camp chores, baiting, tracking wounded bears, and various other duties. Most guides and outfitters want their hunters on stand no later than two or three o'clock in the afternoon. This may seem like a waste of shooting hours, but it's generally because bears have become acclimated to that baiting schedule. Depending on bear activity, and as conditions dictate, some morning hunting may be in the mix, too. If you want to hunt the morning hours, or any other time, don't hesitate to ask. But as a general rule in the dozens of bear camps I've been in over the years, the mornings are free time and the afternoon and evening hours are for actually hunting.

Free time can be spent fishing, lounging around, conversing with fellow hunters, or exploring the area. I like to accompany

In areas with ample water, boats can sometimes be used to reach hunting areas and to retrieve game.

guides on their baiting runs, even helping to bait, and I'm happy to help out around camp if I see a need. Other than breakfast, the biggest meal of the day is usually before hunters depart for the stands. Although I always carry a pee bottle and toilet paper, I try to limit fluid intake two hours before leaving camp on bait hunts and relieve myself before heading out. It simply makes things easier on stand. A smaller meal is served after the hunt, generally long after dark.

Guides usually accompany hunters to the stand each day. Depending on the outfitter, the bait site might have been baited earlier in the day or the guide will do it as the hunter climbs into the stand and gets set. At the end of day, I have had guides tell me to sit tight until they come in and get me, or to meet them on the "main road" at a certain hour, which sometimes means walking long distances after dark.

I have been hunting black bears for a long time, but climbing out of a treestand and following a trail out of the woods in the bear country after the sun goes down still gets me excited. If you aren't comfortable doing this, make sure the guide is aware of it before the hunt. If you decide to walk out on your own, carry a flashlight and make a little noise as you depart the stand. Whistling on the way out will not only ease the nerves a bit, but will make your presence known to any bears still in the area.

TRACKING

The bear hunter's most important job is shot placement, not only for humane reasons but because trailing wounded bears is never fun. Avoid shot angles that don't provide direct access to the vitals. Particularly in the fall, black bears don't bleed as freely as other game animals once hit because of their long coats and the fat layer they have just beneath the skin. In many cases, they won't leave a blood trail until exiting the bait area.

If you're a novice bowhunter, consider using a string tracker. This is basically a reel-like device loaded with line that attaches to the bow. The tag end attaches to the arrow shaft, and on the release, line is dispensed from the reel. There are several string trackers still on the market, and the best ones are loaded with about 2,000 feet of heavy 20- or 22-pound white line. Some are equipped with colored line, but white is easier to follow with flashlights or under low-light conditions. My personal experience has been that string trackers do not affect arrow flight at normal bear hunting range over bait, although archers should practice with them before the hunt.

Hunters using firearms should immediately prepare to get off a second shot if necessary.

Whenever a bear is shot and flees the scene, it's important to listen. On quiet mornings and evenings, elevated stands are great listening and observation posts, and bears generally make a lot of noise as they crash through the woods. Note which direction the bear runs, listening carefully for breaking brush as it goes. If the noise is centered in a specific area, the bear is probably down and dying. And if the sounds stop quickly and everything goes suddenly quiet, chances are the bear is dead, or at least down.

Black bears that are mortally hit and close to death often moan or cough as air is expelled from the lungs, what is generally described as a "death cry." This is a sure indication that the bear is in the process of expiring. The sound isn't pleasant, a bit eerie actually, but it's unmistakable.

If the sound of breaking brush continues for some time after the bear departs, mark the direction of travel and speed as well as you can. Bears that aren't mortally hit will depart quickly and keep moving, but bears hit in the vitals usually slow to a walk or lay down without traveling a great distance. When they do, they often rattle or move brush and small trees. Mark the spot, and continue listening for a few minutes.

Most guides and outfitters will instruct their clients not to track a bear that has been shot, and this is sound advice for novice or inexperienced hunters. If you have any doubts about the hit, or are uncomfortable about following up by yourself, mark the point of exit and direction of travel, and then go find help. But if I'm sure of the hit and confident the bear is down or dead, I like to make at least a quick follow-up if enough daylight remains, although I generally only go fifty to a hundred yards.

If time permits, wait thirty minutes or so and continue to listen carefully before looking for the bear, just like you would with deer. This will allow a hard-hit bear time to expire, or those wounded time to slow down, perhaps even to rest and start to bleed out. If I don't find the bear after following up, I'll return to the area where the bear was shot, mark the direction it departed using surveyor's tape, and either wait until help arrives or go seek it.

Whether to follow up on downed game alone or with the help of a guide is a decision you'll have to make in the field. Pay attention to the bear's direction of travel and listen carefully to help mark its route.

If the guide is relatively sure the bear is dead, based on the hunter's details about the shot, he will often decide to return the same night with a flashlight to take up the pursuit, particularly if rain or snow is in the immediate forecast. Tracking quickly, even in darkness, may provide the best chance of locating the bear.

The faster a dead bear is found and retrieved, the better. Because of its fat and heavy coat, a dead black bear cools very slowly. If it sits too long, particularly in warm weather, the meat and hide may spoil. Quick removal also eliminates the chances that wolves, coyotes, and other scavengers will get to it.

At times, it may be necessary, or deemed best, to track a bear the next morning under full daylight with help from guides, preferably with hounds, if available. This way, an organized and efficient search can be made.

If the bear isn't immediately found, or isn't in the area where it was last heard, search for blood on the ground and on saplings and small trees up to about waist high. Look for tracks or scuff marks on the ground and broken or bent brush. Work slowly and carefully, and search everywhere. A departing bear will often travel through the thickest cover available, and is likely to lie down and expire there, as well.

Once sign or blood has been found, mark the spot with surveyor's tape before moving ahead. If the blood trail is heavy it may not be necessary to mark the trail further, but if blood is scarce mark each spot where blood and other sign is found.

Frothy blood indicates a lung shot, which usually means a short blood trail. Bright blood suggests a heart shot or a severed artery, again a short blood trail. Dark blood means a liver shot. Intestinal matter mixed with blood means a gut shot, and the trail may be quite long. It's best to give gut-shot bears plenty of time to expire before following up. Nonfatal shots may initially leave lots of blood but then taper off; keep looking anyway, crisscrossing the terrain thoroughly.

Wounded bears will often travel downhill or parallel with a ridge when given a choice, and will sometimes seek water. Most bears solidly hit in the vitals with a broadhead or bullet will generally be found within two or three hundred yards, often much closer. Any bear that travels more than a quarter-mile or so without lying down is probably not mortally wounded.

FIELD DRESSING

On outfitted hunts, it's customary for guides to field dress and retrieve bears from the woods, and also to fully skin the animal for transportation home. I enjoy all aspects of the hunt, and make it a point to contribute my share of effort. Every hunter should know how to field dress and care for a bear from start to finish, particularly anyone planning to hunt black bears on their own.

The first decision is whether to dress and skin the animal on the spot. This is normally the way it's done on hound and spot-and-stalk hunts, but on bait hunts many guides and outfitters prefer to do these tasks away from stands, which means the bear will have to be moved. Every guide and experienced bear hunter has

Handling bears is often a two-man game. Here, the guides load bears into a pickup for the trip back to camp.

his own method, but removing the bear from the field is usually done in one of several ways.

If the bear is small, under 150 pounds, it can be carried by one or two people holding onto the legs. I have also carried bears this size out of the woods on my shoulders. Once the weight is properly distributed, it's not too difficult. Larger bears can be tied by the feet to a pole that is then carried by two people. It helps to also secure the bear around the body to prevent it from swaying and catching on brush as it's being moved. In areas where they can be used, ATVs make removal a great deal easier, but the bear should still be tied on securely.

If possible, avoid dragging the bear, but if it's absolutely necessary, drag it head-first using a short length of rope that is attached around the base of the head on one end and to a sturdy stick on the other. This not only keeps the head and heavy front end off the ground, but also pulls the bear with the grain of the hair, which reduces the possibility of damage. The stick allows two people to pull or push at the same time.

Another method is to put a strong stick in the bear's mouth, behind the canines. The mouth is then tied securely shut and the rope secured to each end of the stick for dragging. These tactics usually require more than one person, as getting a bear out of the woods alone can be difficult.

It's sometimes easier to tie larger bears to a pole for transport.

With large black bears, especially when hunting alone or in rough terrain, it's often easier to field dress the animal on the spot. This eliminates fifteen to twenty pounds of dead weight, perhaps more. In some situations, it may also be more convenient to cape the animal in the field rather than back at camp. It depends on the situation, of course, but these tasks are hard to accomplish in the bush.

If the bear is to be mounted, how it will be done should be taken into consideration before field dressing even begins. Also, decide whether the cape is going to be frozen or salted, as freezing greatly reduces the amount of skinning necessary around the head and paws. Take a few pictures for the taxidermist, particularly close-ups of the head from the side and straight on, and of the whole animal, no matter whether you choose a head mount, half- or full-body mount, or rug.

You'll have to fully cape the head if no freezer is available, and it will help the taxidermist achieve a more life-like replica if you take a few basic measurements before starting. These should be from the corner of the eye to the tip of the nose; tip of the nose

Guides usually prefer to field dress and skin bears back at camp, but that's not always possible.

to back of the skull; and the circumference of the neck behind the ears, the chest behind the front legs, and the chest at the last rib. If a full-body mount or rug is desired, measure the bear from the tip of the nose to the base of the tail, and check the circumference of the abdomen in front of the hind legs.

Unless scales are available, this is also a good time to estimate the live weight of the bear. Noted hunting writer and black bear enthusiast Jim Hackiewicz came up with an interesting and

To achieve a life-like mount such as this, the pelt must be properly cared for in the field.

fairly accurate system to do this using body length and chest girth. It's based on a twelve-year study where several hundred black bears were weighed and measured in Washington State. Length is taken from the tip of the nose to the tip of the tail (not the base) and girth around the middle of the bear. The chart is used here with Jim's permission:

ESTIMATING LIVE WEIGHT

	Chest Girth (in inches)		
	66 or less	66–78	78 or more
Body Length (in inches)	Estimated Weight (in pounds)		
29	88	–	–
30	97	–	–
31	105	–	–
32	115	–	–
33	124	–	–
34	134	–	–
35	145	150	–
36	156	170	–
37	167	180	–
38	178	190	–
39	190	210	232
40	203	220	248
41	215	235	263
42	228	255	278
43	241	265	295
44	256	285	312
45	270	300	330
46	284	315	348
47	299	330	385
48	315	250	365
49	330	365	404
50	347	385	424
51	363	400	443
52	380	420	464
53	398	440	486
54	415	460	507
55	433	480	529
56	–	500	551

Chest Girth (in inches)		
66 or less	66–78	78 or more
Body Length (in inches)	**Estimated Weight (in pounds)**	
57	–	520	574
58	–	540	598
59	–	565	623
60	–	585	647

(Dressed weight will be approximately 16 percent less than live weight.)

You can estimate the live weight *after* field dressing by multiplying the dressed weight by 1.16 (the weight of the dressed bear plus 16 percent). For example, if the dressed weight is 200 pounds, the estimated live weight would be around 232 pounds.

Black bears are basically field dressed the same as other big game. First place the animal on its back (belly up), ideally with the head uphill to help with drainage. I like to start at the sternum, at the bottom of the chest bone, and cut through the skin down to just above the pelvis. I make a shallow cut first through the thin outer skin as a guide, which opens up the fat and skin close to the organs and stomach. I didn't know it until I read Richard Smith's *The Book of the Black Bear* back in the late 1980s, but there is a space between the viscera and body-cavity wall just below the sternum that allows you to make a relatively deep cut into the cavity without striking the organs or stomach.

Enter at this point and follow the first cut down the belly through the skin, opening the stomach cavity but making sure not to cut too deeply, which could puncture the paunch. If necessary, use the index and middle fingers on your free hand as a guide and to force down the stomach as you cut. Once this is finished, extend the cut to the pelvis, continuing to use your fingers as a guide.

In some states and provinces, you're required to leave the sex organs intact as proof of gender until the animal is tagged. Once the stomach cavity is open and the organs exposed, cut the diaphragm, the thin skin or muscle separating the chest cavity from the body cavity, severing it as close to the ribs and backbone as possible. Be sure not to slice into the stomach, liver, or intestines as you cut. Roll or push them out of the way as necessary.

Once this is complete, reach into the chest, past the heart and lungs, and up into the neck to grab the windpipe. Pull it tight and cut it off as high as possible. It's often possible to pull the heart and lungs free at this point. Now cut around the anus and remove the lower digestive tract and viscera. It may be necessary to roll the bear on its side to do this, but the entire stomach and chest cavity should empty easily. Check the anal canal for any obstructions and to assist drainage. Clean away any fat or remaining muscle tissue, as well as the kidneys. If the stomach or intestines have been punctured clean away any debris quickly, as this will taint the meat.

The actual skinning can be done in the field or back at camp. Whatever the case, it should be done quickly, the same day as the kill or no later than the next day, especially in warm temperatures. Blowflies, deerflies, and other insects will soon arrive. Female blowflies in particular are quickly drawn to the carcass of dead animals, depositing their eggs in the blood and warm fluids. If the air temperature gets above around sixty degrees Fahrenheit the eggs can hatch quickly, less than a week in some species, and the maggots commence feeding on the flesh, which spoils the meat for human consumption. Prolonged neglect can also cause slippage of the hair.

Rain, snow, and extreme variations in temperature do similar damage, creating or depositing moisture on the carcass and increasing bacterial growth and deterioration. In cool to cold temperatures, bears can actually hang for a day or so, but a warm animal is easier to skin than a cool one.

No matter whether it's done in the field or back at camp, skinning should occur as soon as possible, especially in warm weather.

If you're going to skin the bear in the woods, again place it on its back, but away from where it was dressed to avoid contact with blood and other body fluids. For rug mounts only, make a cut the full length of the body from the tip of the tail to the middle of neck or Adam's apple (see cut 1, figure 9.1). Cutting this high up will provide more hide in the shoulder area, resulting in a rug that's more square and better looking. Cut the rear legs as shown (cut 4), starting or ending at the pads near the toes and extending over the heels. Follow the long hairs or cowlick along the back of the legs to near the anus (where cut 1 began).

The cuts for head mounts, half mounts, and life-size mounts are slightly different, except for the rear feet and legs (cut 4), which remain the same. For head mounts and half mounts, the center cut up the belly (cut 1) should stop slightly below the sternum. This will leave the taxidermist more hide in the brisket area, require less mending, and result in a better mount. Center cuts for life-size mounts should extend slightly higher than the sternum. It's very important to decide what type of mount you

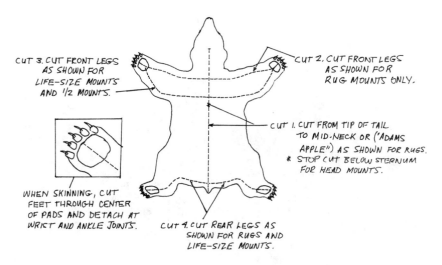

CUT 3. CUT FRONT LEGS
AS SHOWN FOR
LIFE-SIZE MOUNTS
AND 1/2 MOUNTS.

CUT 2. CUT FRONT LEGS
AS SHOWN FOR
RUG MOUNTS ONLY.

CUT 1. CUT FROM TIP OF TAIL
TO MID-NECK OR ("ADAMS
APPLE") AS SHOWN FOR RUGS.
* STOP CUT BELOW STERNUM
FOR HEAD MOUNTS.

WHEN SKINNING, CUT
FEET THROUGH CENTER
OF PADS AND DETACH AT
WRIST AND ANKLE JOINTS.

CUT 4. CUT REAR LEGS AS
SHOWN FOR RUGS AND
LIFE-SIZE MOUNTS.

Fig. 9.1. Basic cuts for skinning.

want before making these cuts, because it determines where the front legs are cut and where they intersect with the center cut.

For rugs, the cut should run along the back of the front legs (cut 2), starting or ending partway into the pads forward of the wrists, and extend to the center cut (cut 1) in the middle of the chest area. For head mounts, half mounts, and full mounts, however, the cut should run along the back of the legs, following the long hair or cowlick, and intersect with the center cut at one of the points indicated in the paragraph above.

Now the actual skinning can commence, either in the stomach area or on the legs. If you start at the stomach, roll the bear as needed to reach the backbone, using your free hand to work and pull the hide from the carcass as you cut. (This is easier if a companion grips the front or rear leg and rolls the carcass as you cut.) Make sure to free the pelt over the hindquarters and front shoulders when you do each side.

When one side is complete, spread the freed hide out on the ground and roll the carcass onto it to keep it clean. Work on the

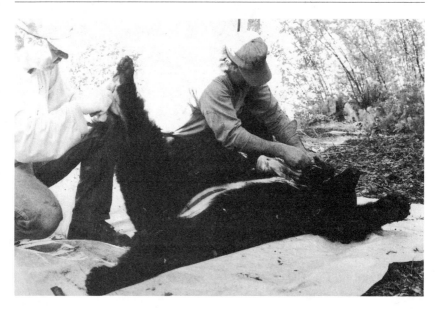

The initial skinning cut is from anus to brisket. Having an extra set of hands is helpful.

other side until the stomach area is completely detached. When you do the front legs, cut fully around them, and when you reach the pads, skin as far as the wrist and sever the connecting tissue and muscle at the joint. A bone saw works well here, but be careful not to slice the hide. At the rear pads, cut to the toes and cut at the joints. If you're short on time, the rear feet can be severed at the ankle joint.

The head is next. To save time in the field, skin up the neck to the base of the skull, or as far as possible, pulling the pelt if necessary, and sever the neck at that point. Skinning the rest of the head can be done back at camp under better conditions. The entire pelt should now be free from the carcass. Quarter the animal, taking the meat from the shoulders, unless severely damaged, the hindquarters, and the loins and tenderloins— just like a deer—and prepare it for transport back to camp or the vehicle. The ribs are generally fatty, but there is some meat on them, as

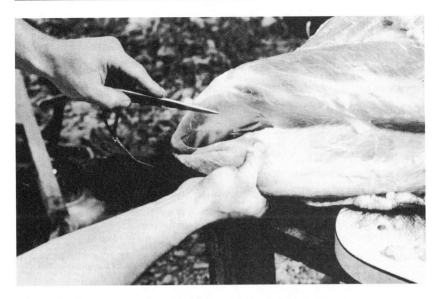

It's usually okay to stop at the ankle as you work down the leg.

well as on the neck if you have the time and want to bother with it. If I'm skinning and quartering in the field, I usually pass on this, but when working from camp I do take the neck meat, which makes good stews.

The quarters and meat are best wrapped in cheesecloth to keep them clean and to allow rapid cooling. Carry them out of the woods on a pack frame or in a backpack. If you must use plastic bags, remove the meat as quickly as

If you're working in the field, the feet can be cut off and skinned later back at camp.

possible to prevent the meat from overheating and spoiling. To transport the pelt, fold the feet into the middle, followed by the head, and then roll or fold it to form a neat bundle, fur side out. If necessary, wrap it with rope or twine to keep it all together. Some hunters and guides simply drape the pelt over the shoulder or around the neck like a blanket.

If the bear has been removed for skinning back at camp, it can be hung from a game pole by the hind feet. This makes skinning easier and helps keep the pelt clean. If the temperature is cool, less than forty-five degrees or so, the bear can hang for a day or two if necessary, as long as it's in the shade and kept dry. Check for flies often, and keep in mind that direct sunlight will spoil the meat and start to degrade the pelt as quickly as moisture will. No matter where you do it, skinning the bear as quickly as possible is always best.

Proper skinning in the head area is critical for a good mount. Only experienced guides and hunters should tackle this job.

Hanging the bear back at camp before skinning makes it much easier to keep the pelt clean as you work.

What happens next depends on whether a freezer is available. If it is, the pelt can be stowed as is in a plastic bag until you depart for home. It should be kept cold or frozen until delivered to the taxidermist with your measurements and photographs. The taxidermist will finish skinning the head.

The meat can simply be frozen too, but it's easier to first remove all fat, blood-shot meat, hair, and dirt and to de-bone the meat. Once the meat is clean and de-boned, it should be kept cool or frozen for shipment home.

If freezers or coolers aren't available, you'll have to fully skin the head and paws. This is critical, and it's important to take extra care around the eyes, leaving the tear ducts and lids and the lips and gums. When you get to the nose, cut the cartilage half to three-quarters of an inch back from the tip, keeping the nostrils fully intact.

The ears must also be turned and fully skinned. Carefully skin or cut out the ear butt and separate the ear from the cartilage to the tip. The feet must be fully skinned, as well. Next, clean away any fat or tissue, leave everything inside out, especially the ears, and thoroughly salt the pelt, working the salt into the head,

This close-up of a head mount shows how proper skinning around the mouth pays off. If this area isn't handled skillfully, there's only so much a taxidermist can do to fix it.

lips, mouth, and ears. Use non-iodized salt only, such as pickling salt. (Do not use rock salt or common iodized salt.) It should take 20 to 25 pounds of salt for a 150- to 200-pound black bear. Roll the pelt hair side out, put it in a cool place, and allow the salt to work overnight. Check it the next day, and, if necessary, remove the wet salt and reapply as needed. Continue to allow it to air dry in a cool place.

These two pelts are ready to be squared, then salted or frozen.

Salted pelts should be hung in a cool place to air dry.

If the bear was harvested early in the week and has fully cooled and sufficiently drained, store the pelt in a cloth bag and ship it home in a wax-lined cardboard box or cooler. Get it to the taxidermist as soon as possible. If the bear was taken late in the week, the salt will still be working on the pelt during the trip home. In this case, it's best to pack the pelt in ice. But water and moisture must be kept off the skin. Place ice in a separate plastic bag or make ice blocks using milk containers or soda bottles. On outfitted hunts, the guides are well versed in all skinning and packing procedures, but hunters doing it themselves should take extra precautions, perhaps even consulting with a taxidermist before the hunt.

ON THE TABLE

One of the reasons I hunt black bears is because I love bear meat, especially the loins and tenderloins, which are excellent when marinated and cooked on a hot grill. The neck meat makes great stews, and the hams and shoulders good roasts. Leftover cuts, even meat on the ribs, can be made into sausage. Like most big game, the nutritive value of black bear meat surpasses that of commercially produced beef. It's high in protein, minerals, and vitamins and low in fat and calories. It's simply great stuff.

For the best taste, bear meat must be properly cared for in the field and thoroughly cooked. Aging bear meat isn't necessary. It doesn't improve flavor or tenderness, and tends to dry meat out and make it tougher. All fat, or as much fat as possible, should be removed. Also, try to freeze, can, or consume the meat within a week of harvesting, since it becomes stronger with age.

Freezer life is about six months at minus ten degrees, and perhaps up to nine months at minus twenty, provided the meat is properly wrapped—preferably double wrapped or vacuum-sealed.

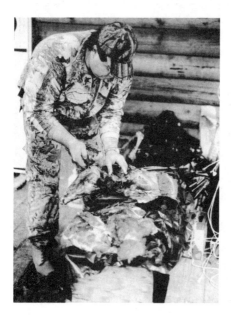

Bear meat can carry the parasite *Trichinella spiralis*, which causes trichinosis. The meat is safe to eat if cooked at 375 degrees Fahrenheit for twenty to twenty-five minutes per pound. For cuts much larger than three pounds it's best to double the cooking time. A temperature of 137

This hunter is preparing his meat for shipment home. Bear meat is excellent on the table if it's handled properly afield.

degrees actually kills the parasite, but according to the USDA, a safer margin is cooking the meat until it has an internal roasting temperature of 170 degrees. A good rule of thumb is to cook all bear meat, including steaks on the grill, until there is no trace of pink meat or fluid. Freezing doesn't kill the parasite, nor does cooking in a microwave oven.

Most wild-game cookbooks have recipes for bear meat, but it can generally be flavored the same as pork.

Appendix

BEAR HUNTING RESOURCES

STATE AND PROVINCE CONTACT INFORMATION

(Season dates are for 2004; always check for updated regulations before planning a trip.)

ALASKA

Season
- Year-round in some areas; check desired hunting units
- Baiting and hounds allowed

Department of Fish and Game
Division of Wildlife Conservation
Box 25526
Juneau, AK 99802
907-465-4190
www.adfg.state.ak.us

ARIZONA

Season
- March 19–May 20
- April 28–September 27 (archery only)
- August 22–December 31
- Hounds allowed

Arizona Game and Fish Department
2222 West Greenway Road
Phoenix, AZ 85023
602-942-3000
www.azgfd.com

ARKANSAS

Season
- October 1–December 21
- Baiting allowed on private land

Arkansas Game and Fish Commission
2 Natural Resources Drive
Little Rock, AR 72205
501-223-6351
www.agfc.com

CALIFORNIA

Season
- August 9–September 7
- September 15–December 28
- Hounds allowed

California Department of Fish and Game
3211 S Street
Sacramento, CA 95816
916-227-2271
www.dfg.ca.gov

COLORADO

Season
- September 2–November 30

• Spot-and-stalk only

Colorado Division of Wildlife
6060 Broadway
Denver, CO 80216
303-291-7529
www.dnr.state.co.us

GEORGIA

Season
• September 13–November 23
• Hounds allowed in some areas

Georgia Wildlife Resources Division
2111 US Highway 278
Social Circle, GA 30025
770-918-6416
www.dnr.state.ga.us

IDAHO

Season
• April 1–June 30
• August 30–October 31
• Baiting and hounds allowed

Idaho Fish and Game Department
600 South Walnut
Boise, ID 83707
208-334-3700
www.state.id.us/fishgame

MAINE

Season
- August 25–November 29
- Baiting and hounds allowed

Maine Department of Inland Fisheries and Wildlife
41 State House Station
284 State Street
Augusta, ME 04333
207-287-8000
www.state.me.us/ifw

MASSACHUSETTS

Season
- September 2–November 25
- Spot-and-stalk only

Massachusetts Department of Natural Resources
Wildlife Division
100 Cambridge Street/Room 1902
Boston, MA 02202
617-727-3151
www.state.ma.us/dfwele

MICHIGAN

Season
- September 10–October 26
- Baiting and hounds allowed

Michigan Department of Natural Resources
Wildlife Division
P.O. Box 30444

Lansing, MI 58909
517-373-1263
www.michigan.gov/dnr

MINNESOTA
Season
• September 1–October 12
• Baiting allowed

Minnesota Department of Natural Resources
500 Lafayette Road
St. Paul, MN 55155
651-296-6157
www.dnr.state.mn.us

MONTANA
Season
• April 15–May 31
• September 15–November 20
• Spot-and-stalk only

Montana Department of Fish, Wildlife, and Parks
P.O. Box 200701
Helena, MT 59620
406-444-2535
www.fwp.state.mt.us

NEW HAMPSHIRE
Season
• September 1–December 8
• Baiting and hounds allowed

New Hampshire Fish and Game Department
2 Hazen Drive
Concord, NH 03301
603-271-3422
www.wildlife.state.nh.us

NEW JERSEY

Season
- December 8–13
- Spot-and-stalk only

New Jersey Division of Fish and Wildlife
P.O. Box 400
Trenton, NJ 08625
609-292-2965
www.state.nj.us/dep/fgw/bear

NEW MEXICO

Season
- August 1–November 15
- Hounds allowed

New Mexico Game and Fish Department
P.O. Box 25112
Santa Fe, NM 87504
505-476-8000
www.gmfh.state.nm.us

NEW YORK

Season
- September 14–December 17
- Spot-and-stalk only

New York Department of Environmental Conservation
50 Wolf Road, Room 151
Albany, NY 12233
518-457-3521
www.dec.state.ny.us

NORTH CAROLINA

Season
• October 14–January 1
• Hounds allowed

North Carolina Wildlife Resources Commission
512 N. Salisbury Street
Raleigh, NC 27604
919-733-7291
www.ncwildlife.org

OREGON

Season
• April 15–June 23
• August 1–December 31
• Spot-and-stalk only

Oregon Department of Fish and Wildlife
P.O. Box 59
Portland, OR 97207
503-947-6000
www.dfw.state.or.us

PENNSYLVANIA

Season
• November 24–December 6

- Spot-and-stalk only

Pennsylvania Game Commission
2001 Elmerton Avenue
Harrisburg, PA 17110
717-787-2084
www.pgc.state.pa.us

SOUTH CAROLINA

Season
- October 21–November 2
- Hounds allowed

South Carolina Department of Natural Resources
P.O. Box 167
Columbia, SC 29202
803-734-3886
www.dnr.state.sc.us

TENNESSEE

Season
- September 29–December 17
- Hounds allowed

Tennessee Wildlife Resources Agency
P.O. Box 40747
Nashville, TN 37202
615-781-6615
www.state.tn.us

UTAH

Season

- April 13–May 27
- August 1–November 27
- Baiting and hounds allowed

Utah State Department of Natural Resources
Division of Wildlife Resources
1596 W. North Temple
Salt Lake City, UT 84114
801-538-4700
www.wildlife.utah.gov

VERMONT
Season
- September 1–November 19
- Hounds allowed

Vermont Fish and Wildlife Department
103 S. Main Street
Waterbury, VT 05671
802-241-3700
www.anr.state.vt.us/fw

VIRGINIA
Season
- October 11–January 30
- Hounds allowed

Virginia Department of Game and Inland Fisheries
P.O. Box 11104
Richmond, VA 23230
804-367-9369
www.dgif.state.va.us

WASHINGTON

Season

- July 16–November 15
- Spot-and-stalk only

Washington Department of Fish and Wildlife
600 Capital Way North
Olympia, WA 98501
360-902-2200
www.wa.gov/wdfw

WEST VIRGINIA

Season

- October 12–December 31
- Hounds allowed

West Virginia Division of Natural Resources
1900 Kanawha Avenue East
Building 3, Room 624
Charleston, WV 25305
304-558-3399
www.wvweb.com/www/hunting

WISCONSIN

Season

- September 13–October 7
- Baiting and hounds allowed

Wisconsin Department of Natural Resources
P.O. Box 7921
Madison, WI 53707
608-266-2621

www.dnr.state.wi.us

WYOMING

Season
- April 1–June 15
- August 1–November 15
- Baiting allowed

Wyoming Game and Fish Department
5400 Bishop Boulevard
Cheyenne, WY 82006
307-777-4600
www.gf.state.wy.us

ALBERTA

Season
- April 1–May 31
- August 25–November 30
- Baiting allowed

Alberta Wildlife Management Division
Main Floor, North Tower
Petroleum Plaza
9945 108th Street
Edmonton, AL T5K 2G6
780-427-5185
www3.gov.ab.ca

BRITISH COLUMBIA

Season
- Year-round; check for details
- Hounds allowed

British Columbia Ministry of the Environment, Lands, and Parks
Wildlife Branch
780 Blanchard Street
Victoria, BC V8V 1X4
250-387-9711
www.gov.bc.ca/walp

MANITOBA

Season
- April 22–June 22
- August 26–October 5
- Baiting allowed

Manitoba Natural Resources
200 Salteaux Crescent
Winnipeg, MB R3J 3W3
204-945-6784
www.gov.mb.ca/natres/wildlife

NEW BRUNSWICK

Season
- April 21–June 28
- September 8–November 1
- Baiting allowed

New Brunswick Department of Natural Resources
Fish and Wildlife Division
P.O. Box 6000
Fredericton, NB E3B 5H1
506-453-2440
www.gbn.ca

NEWFOUNDLAND/LABRADOR
Season
- Year-round; check for details
- Baiting allowed

Newfoundland/Labrador Department of Tourism
Wildlife Division
P.O. Box 8700
St. John's, NF A1B 4J6
709-637-2007
www.gov.nf.ca/tourism

NORTHWEST TERRITORIES
Season
- August 15–June 30
- Spot-and-stalk only

Northwest Territories
Wildlife, Economic Development
P.O. Box 2668
Yellowknife, NT X1A 2P9
867-669-2388
www.nwtwildlife.rwed.gov.nt.ca

NOVA SCOTIA
Season
- September 8–December 6
- Baiting and hounds allowed

Nova Scotia Department of Natural Resources
P.O. Box 698
Halifax, NS B3J 2T9

902-679-6140
www.gov.ns.ca/natr

ONTARIO

Season

- August 15–November 30
- Baiting and hounds allowed

Ontario Natural Resources Information Center
1st Floor, P.O. Box 7000
300 Water Street
Peterborough, ON K9J 3C7
705-235-1157
www.mnr.gov.on.ca/mnr/pubs

QUEBEC

Season

- May 15–June 30
- August 25–October 31
- Baiting allowed

Quebec Department of Recreation
Fish and Wildlife Division
150 Rene Levesque E., 4th Floor
Quebec City, PQ G1R 4Y1
418-842-0318
www.gouv.qc.ca/publications

SASKATCHEWAN

Season

- April 14–June 28
- August 21–October 11

• Baiting allowed

Saskatchewan Environmental Resource Management
Wildlife Branch, Room 436
3211 Albert Street
Regina, SK S4S 5W6
306-787-2314

YUKON
Season
• April 15–June 21
• August 1–November 15
• Spot-and-stalk only

Yukon Renewable Resources
Field Service Branch
P.O. Box 2703
Whitehorse, YK Y1A 2C6
867-667-5221
www.environmentyukon.gov.yk.ca

OUTFITTERS AND GUIDES ASSOCIATIONS

Alaska Professional Hunters Association
P.O. Box 91932
Anchorage, AK 99509
907-522-3221
www.alaskaprohunter.org

Colorado Outfitters Association
P.O. Box 1949
Rifle, CO 81650

970-876-9543
www.colorado-outfitters.com

New Mexico Council of Outfitters and Guides
P.O. Box 93186
Albuquerque, NM 87199
505-822-9808
www.nmoutfitters.org

Idaho Outfitters and Guides Association
P.O. Box 95
Boise, ID 83701
208-338-7830
www.ioga.org

Wyoming Outfitters and Guides Association
P.O. Box 2284
Cody, WY 82414
307-527-7453
www.wyoga.org

Professional Recreation Outfitters of Wyoming
P.O. Box 2697
Cheyenne, WY 82003

Maine Professional Guides Association
P.O. Box 847
Augusta, ME 04332
207-785-2061
www.maineguides.org

Montana Outfitters and Guides Association
P.O. Box 1248
Helena, MT 59620
406-449-3578
www.moga-montana.org

Nevada Outfitters Association
P.O. Box 135
Wells, NV 89835
775-777-3277

New York State Outdoor Guides Association
P.O. Box 916
Saranac, NY 12983
518-359-7037
www.nysoga.com

Washington Outfitters Association
709 228th Avenue NE, Suite 331
Redmond, WA 98053
425-392-0111

Alberta Professional Outfitters Society
#103, 6030 88 Street
Edmonton, AB T6E 6G4
780-414-0249
www.apos.ab.ca

Professional Outfitters Association of Alberta
P.O. Box 67012
Meadowlark Park Post Office
Edmonton, AB T5R 5Y3

Outfitters Association of British Columbia
P.O. Box 94675
Richmond, BC V6Y 4A4
604-278-2688
www.goabc.org

Yukon Outfitters Association
P.O. Box 4548
Whitehorse, Yukon Y1A 2R8
867-668-4118
www.yukonoutfitters.net

Manitoba Lodges and Outfitters Association
23 Sage Street
Winnipeg, MB R2Y 0X8
204-889-4840
www.mloa.com

New Brunswick Outfitters Association
P.O. Box 74
Woodstock, NB E0J 2B0
1-800-215-2075
www.nboa.nb.ca

Newfoundland/Labrador Outfitters Association
107 LeMerchant Road
St. John's, NF A1C 2H1
www.nloa.ca

Federation of Outfitters
5237 Hamel Boulevard, Local 270
Quebec City, PQ G2E 2H2

418-521-3880

www.fpq.com

Saskatchewan Outfitters Association
3700 2nd Avenue W
Prince Rupert, SA S6W 1A2
306-763-5434
www.soa.com

MAGAZINES

Bear Hunting Magazine
P.O. Box 457
Becker, MN 55308
877-420-2327
www.bearhunting.com

American Hunter
11250 Waples Mill Road
Fairfax, VA 22030
703-267-1000
www.nrapublications.org

North American Hunting
www.huntingclub.com

Outdoor Life
Subscription Services
P.O. Box 60001
Tampa, FL 33660

1-800-365-1580
www.outdoorlife.com

Field & Stream
2 Park Avenue
New York, NY 10016
www.fieldandstream.com

Bowhunting World
6420 Sycamore Lane N.
Maple Grove, MN 55369
815-734-1285
www.bowhuntingworld.com

Bowhunter
6405 Flank Drive
Harrisburg, PA 17112
717-657-9555
bowhunter@primediamags.com

Petersen's Hunting and *Petersen's Bowhunting*
www.huntingmag.com

Bow and Arrow Hunting
Y-Visionary Publishing
265 S. Anita Drive
Suite 120
Orange, CA 92868
www.bowandarrowhunting.com

Hunting Illustrated
King's Outdoor World

P.O. Box 307
11355 East 16000 North
Mt. Pleasant, UT 84647
www.huntingillustrated.com

Blackpowder Hunting
P.O. Box 1180
Glen Rock, WY 82637
307-436-9817
www.blackpowderhunting.org

Big Game Adventures
P.O. Box 29099, OK Mission RPO
Kelowna, BC V1W 4AZ
Canada
1-866-944-8382
www.biggameadventures.com

Selected Bibliography

Barnes Reloading Manual, No. 2. American Fork, Utah: Barnes Bullets, Inc., 1997.

Black Bear in Modern North America. Kalispell, Mont.: Boone and Crockett Club, 1977.

Boddington, Craig. *Shots at Big Game.* Long Beach, Cal.: Safari Books, 1989.

Brakefield, Tom. *Hunting Big-Game Trophies.* New York: Outdoor Life/Dutton, 1976.

Cox, Daniel, J. *Black Bear.* San Francisco: Chronicle Books, 1989.

Domico, Terry. *Bears of the World.* New York: Facts on File, 1988.

Fadala, Sam. *The Complete Blackpowder Handbook.* Iola, Wis.: DBI Books, 1996.

Fair, Jeff and Lynn Rogers. *The Great American Bear.* Minocqua, Wis.: NorthWord Press, Inc., 1990.

Godin, Alfred, J. *Wild Mammals of New England.* Baltimore: The John Hopkins University Press, 1977.

Hodgdon Date Manual No. 26. Shawnee Mission, Kan.: Hodgdon Power Company, 1994.

Lee Rue III, Leonard. *Furbearing Animals of North America.* New York: Crown Publishers, 1981.

Nesbitt, William H. and Philip L. Wright. *Measuring and Scoring North American Big Game Trophies.* Boone and Crockett Club, 1985.

Ormond, Clyde. *Complete Book of Hunting.* New York: Outdoor Life/Harper & Row, 1962.

Raychard, Al. *The Ultimate Guide to Blackpowder Hunting.* Guilford, Conn.: The Lyons Press, 2001.

Rezendes, Paul. *Tracking and the Art of Seeing, How to Read Animal Tracks and Sign.* Charlotte, Vt.: Camden House Publishing, 1992.

Smith, Richard. *The Book of the Black Bear.* Piscataway, NJ: Winchester Press, 1985.

Wildlife Management Techniques. Washington, D.C.: The Wildlife Society, 1971.

Index

A
Agricultural crops, 38
Alaska
    bag limits, 73
    black bear hunting
        season, 199
    outfitters and guides
        associations, 265
    state contact information,
        251
Alberta, 15
    bag requirements, 75–76
    black bear photos, 147,
        166
    color-phase black bear
        photo, 155
    outfitters and guides
        associations, 267
    province contact
        information, 261
America's bear, 9–30
Animal rights groups, 74
Aperture sights, 139
Appalachians, 18
Arizona
    state contact information,
        251–252
Arkansas
    bait requirements, 71
    state contact information,
        252
Armguard, 166
Arrow
    material, 163
    selection, 159–167
    tips, 164–166
    weight
        determining, 163
Attractants
    grease and oils, 91–93
    placement, 92
Ayers, Don, 15

B
Backtrack, 111
Bag limits
    variations, 73
Baiting, 77–108
    amounts for, 85, 86, 89,
        90, 91
    Canada allowed areas, 78
    containers, 95–98
    regulations, 95
    securing, 97

types, 97
    cost, 212
    establishing productive
        sites, 211
    food for, 84–98
    hole, 95
    hunts
        cost, 111
        importance of variety, 89,
            90
        placement, 80–84
        plus adding scent, 93
            photo, 94
        pros and cons, 78–80
        in reference to water, 83
        schedules, 98–100
            consistency
                importance, 99, 100,
                    102
        states allowed, 77
        treestand location, 104
        when to hunt, 82–83
Ball starter, 183
Barks per minute, 111
Bawl mouth, 111
Baying, 111
Bear Bait, 94
Bear Call Lure, 94
Bear Focus Call, 94
Bear Focus Lure, 94
Bear Scents, 93
Beaver carcasses
    for baiting, 85
Beef parts
    for baiting, 84–85
Behavior
    sex determination, 63
Belly
    size vs. age, 59–60
Belly hair
    sex determination, 62
Binoculars, 123–124
Birdsong, George F.L., 116–117
Bitch, 112
Black and tan hounds, 116
Black bears
    activity vs. outside
        temperature, 207, 208
    age determination, 58–60
    best time to harvest, 20
    camp, 222–230
        packing list, 224–226
        remote site
            transportation, 225

type, 222
    colorations, 14–18
    estimating live weight,
        237–238
    euphemisms, 3
    feeding styles, 80
    field removal, 234
        pole transport, 235
    gait, 51–52
    harvested yearly, 6
        mandatory check-ins, 75
    heaviest recorded wild
        male, 17
    hunting
        Canada and US areas,
            75
    hunting initiatives
        political involvement,
            74
    hunting resources,
        251–271
        magazines, 269–271
        outfitters, 265–269
        state and province
            contact information,
                251–265
    identification signs,
        69–70
    illustrated drawing, 69
    licenses
        availability, 72
    lineages, 12
    metabolism rate, 32
    photo, 11, 18, 24, 41, 180
        Alberta, 147, 166
        boar, 20, 34
        Canada, 202
        cub, 59
        field removal, 234
        Idaho, 136, 167, 175
        Maine, 149, 198, 213
        Manitoba, 150, 165
        mounted, 236
        New Brunswick, 137,
            206
        Newfoundland, 148,
            181
        Quebec, 208
        spring, 204
        white markings, 14
    record book minimums,
        64
    reputation, 6–7
    searching for food, 38

Black bears *(continued)*
  seasons, 197–210
    in Canada, 200
    fall, 207–210
    spring, 200–206
    in US, 199
  sex determination, 61–63
  sightings
    scouting tool, 41
  size determination, 58–60
  species and subspecies,
    10, 12–13
    marking and color,
    14–15
    range area, 13
  squaring procedure, 51
  targets for practice,
    158–159
  toe and nail, or claw,
    lengths, 52–53
  tree usage, 55
  woods, 31–70
  wounded
    tracking procedure,
    230–233
Blackpowder, 170
  helpful items, 183
  size, 181–182
Blanketback, 112
Blood
  importance of color and
    consistency when
    tracking, 233
Bloodline, 112
Blue Hill area of Maine, 16
Bluetick, 116
  photo, 115
Boars
  black bear photo, 20, 34
  identification, 61–63
  vs. sow
    head, 58–59
    hibernation period, 25
    hibernation period
      ending, 210
    size, 19
Body length
  chest girth
    estimating live weight,
    237–238
Body shape
  trophy caliber, 60
Body temperature, 26
Book of the Black Bear, 238
Boots
  hound hunting, 120
Bow

selection, 159–167
Bowhunting, 153–167
  aiming point, 156
  bear season
    state or province, 167
  helpful items, 166
  string tracker, 230
Bowstring silencers, 166
Box dog, 112
Brakefield, Tom, 58
Breaking scent, 112
Breeding season, 62
British Columbia, 12
  outfitters and guides
    associations, 268
  province contact
    information, 261–262
Broadheads, 164–166
  cutting edges, 165
  grain range, 165
  manufacturers list, 166
  presharpened, 165
Broadside shot, 141
  and bowhunting, 155–156
  illustrated, 142, 143
Broke dog, 112
Brood bitch, 112
Bullet
  hollowpoint, 151
  shape, 150
  velocity and resistance,
    147
  weights
    list, 151–152

C
Cabral, Joe, 11, 15, 87–88
Caliber
  definition, 147
  selection, 131, 145–152
California
  bait requirements, 71–72
  state contact information,
    252
Calling
  types used, 129
Cam operated compound bow,
  159
Canada. *See also* individual
    provinces
  bag limits, 73
  black bear hunting
    season, 200
  gun registration
    requirements, 221
  population, 29–30
Canned dog food

  for baiting, 88
Canoes
  and bear hunting, 125–126
Caplock reproduction
  muzzleloaders, 172
Cappers, 183, 184
Carbon arrow, 164
Carrion
  for baiting, 84–85
Cartridges, 131–152
  round or flat nose, 150
  selection, 145–152
Cat foot, 112
CB radios
  hound hunting, 119–120
Cedar arrows, 164
Changeover bark, 112
Check dog, 112
Check in, 112
Chest girth
  body length
    estimating live weight,
    237–238
Chicken
  for baiting, 84–85
Claws
  photo, 28
Clearwater National Forest, 15
Climbing portable stand, 105
Close hunter, 112
Clothing
  hound hunting, 120
  scent eliminating
    activated carbon
    clothing, 103
Cold calling, 129
Cold nose, 112
Colorado
  bait requirements, 71–72
  outfitters and guides
    associations, 265–266
  state contact information,
    252–253
  voter passed regulations,
    73–74
Colored black bears, 14–18
Color-phase black bears, 14–18
  photo, 16
  Alberta, 155
  trophy value, 66
Compound bow
  advantages, 159
  arrow velocity, 154
  manufacturers list, 161
  photo, 154
  pulleys *vs.* cam, 159–160
Conical bullets, 173

caliber *vs.* weight, 177
  energy and velocity, 177
  manufacturers list, 178
  photo, 178
  proper powder charge, 179
  range limitations, 173
Contender
  barrel length, 194
  caliber options, 194
  photo, 194
Coonhounds
  photo, 117
Coordinated drives, 122, 130
Corn on cob
  for baiting, 88–89
Crosshairs, 138

D
Dam, 113
Dead tree, 114
Death cry, 231
Demeanor, 23
Dew claws, 113
Diet
  composed of, 36
Digs
  scouting tool, 57
Distribution, 27, 28
Donuts
  for baiting, 86
Dot, 138
Double-lung shot
  and bowhunting, 157
Downed game
  tracking, 230–233
Draw length
  determining, 162
Draw weight
  adjusting, 160–161
  match with arrow,
    162–163
  suggested settings, 161
Dressed weight
  estimating live weight, 238
Droppings. *See* Scat
Dry dog food
  for baiting, 88

E
Ears
  skinning procedure, 245
Easton Gamegetter II 2216
  arrow, 163–164
Electronic calls, 129–130
Encore
  barrel length, 194
  caliber options, 194

photo, 194
Energy needed
  bullet delivers, 148
  conical bullets, 177
  in foot-pounds, 145–146
English foxhounds, 116
Excretion, 34
Expanding bullets, 178
Eyes
  and using scope, 139

F
Fair, Jeff, 10
Fall seasons, 207–210
  bear activity
    optimum conditions,
      208
  bear size, 206
  breeding, 209
  Canadian provinces
    allow, 200
  feeding frenzy, 209
  food supply, 208
  insects, 207
  pelt condition, 207
  states that allow, 199
  weather conditions
    bear activity, 207
Farmers
  scouting tool, 41
Fawn bleats, 130
Feeding season, 38
  fall, 39
Feet
  skinning procedure, 245
Females. *See* Sows
Fiber-optic sight system
  muzzleloaders, 174
Fiduccia, Peter, 213
Field dressing, 233–247
  feet, 243
  legs, 243
  mounting type
    determines steps, 235
  procedure, 238–246
  illustration, 241
  photo, 240
  and salting, 246
  tagging regulations, 238
  and temperature concern,
    244
Finished hound, 113
Firearms
  selection, 131
Fish
  for baiting, 84–85
Fixed scopes, 137–138

Flintlock muzzleloaders, 171
  photo, 171
Florida black bear, 12
Food, 9, 10, 32–43
  for baiting, 84–98
  consumed determined by
    scat, 44–45
  favorite, 37
  hunting for, 23
  movement factor, 39
  scouting tool, 9, 11, 35
  sources, 35
  spring and summer, 33
  variety, 11
Foot
  hind *vs.* front, 49
Fort McMurray, 15
Foster-type rifled slug, 186
Four-blade broadhead, 165
4-in-1 T-Loader, 183–184
Foxhounds
  photo, 117
Freeze brand, 113
French hounds, 116
Frizzen, 171
Front foot
  and squared hide size
    determination, 49
  tracks, 48
Fruits, 9. *See also* Food
  for baiting, 88–89
Full cry, 113
Full size 3-D targets, 158–159

G
Gait, 51–52
  size determination, 60
Georgia
  state contact information,
    253
Gestation period, 21
Glassing, 9, 40
Glove, 166
Grains
  for baiting, 88
Great American Bear, 10
Great Bear, 5–6
Grizzly bear, 12, 66–69
  identification signs, 68–69
  illustrated drawing, 69
  last known killed, 67
  recovery zones, 68
  reintroduction, 67
  scat, 46
Ground blinds, 106
  location selection, 107
Guard fur, 19–20

Guard hair, 19
Guide
  choosing, 214–222
  confirming dates in
    advance, 221
  list, 265–269
  vs. outfitters, 218
Gyp, 113

H
Habitat, 19
  understanding, 31–32
Hackiewicz, Jim, 236
Hair
  scouting tool, 57
Half mounts
  skinning procedure,
    240–242
Handgun hunting, 189–196
  bullet selection, 190, 195
  caliber selection, 192–193
    important, 191
  cartridges, 191, 192
    suggested, 193, 196
  .454
    range, 193–194
  impact velocity needed,
    190
  photo, 190
  range limitation, 192, 193
  velocity importance, 189
    amount needed, 190
  wildcat and big-bore
    calibers, 194–195
Hard cast bullets, 195
Head
  boar vs. sow, 58–59
  mounts
    skinning procedure,
      240–242
  size vs. age, 58–59
  skinning procedure, 245
Head-on shots, 144
Head shots, 141
  and bowhunting, 156
Hearing, 23–24
Heart shots, 141
  illustrated, 142, 143
Hering, Brad, 93–94
Hibernation period, 19, 24–25
  boar vs. sow, 25
  ending, 210
  length and duration, 25
  triggered by, 25
Hind foot
  tracks, 48
Hole baits, 95

Hollowpoints, 195
Honey
  for baiting, 87
Honey and bees, 38
Honey burn, 87–88
Hornady, William, 15
Hot nose, 113
Hound hunting
  Canada allowed areas, 78
  chase, 117–122
  choosing breed, 114–117
  cost, 109, 111
  day packing items, 226
  desired characteristic of
    hound, 110
  electronic tracking
    equipment, 120
  history, 109
  lingo, 111–114
  owning and running,
    108–109
  packages, 213
  physical endurance,
    226–228
  raising and breeding,
    108–109
  states allowed, 77
Human scent
  pros and cons, 102–104
Hunt
  fascination with, 3
  finding place, 212
  first experience, 1–3
  location
    determine gear
      requirements, 223
  planning, 211–249
    gun registration
      requirements, 221
    outfitters vs. guides, 213
    physical shape, 226–228
Hunters
  ability to identify bear
    species, 67–68
  numbers of, 6
Hunting Big-Game Trophies,
  58
Hunting methods, 71–130
  baiting
    less physically
      demanding, 228
    with hounds, 108–122
    physically demanding,
      228
    restrictions, 75
  least expensive, 213–214
  remote areas, 216

state, provincial, and
    territorial wildlife
    agencies
    contacts, 251–265
  control regulations,
    71–72
  with hounds, 77, 78
  legalities, 76–77
  over bait, 77, 78
  stop and stalk techniques
    physically demanding,
      228
  use all senses, 125
  weapon variation, 72
Hyperphagia, 25

I
Idaho, 15
  bag limits, 73
  black bear photos, 136,
    167, 175
  grizzly bear, 67
  outfitters and guides
    associations, 266
  state contact information,
    253
  voter passed regulations,
    73–74
Ignition systems
  types, 171–175
Ill dog, 113
Information source, 39–40
In-line muzzleloaders, 171
  capper, 185
    photo, 185
  cap remover, 185
  design types, 173–175
    photo, 175
  propellant needed, 180
  rifle twists, 174
  scopes, 186
Iroquois legend of The Three
  Bears, 5–6

J
Jacketed bullets
  caliber vs. weight, 177
  manufacturers list, 178
Jacobson's organ, 24
Junk game, 113

K
Knight muzzleloader
  photo, 181

L
Labrador

outfitters and guides
associations, 268
province contact
information, 263
Ladder stands, 105
cost, 105
Legends, 3–7
Legs
size *vs.* age, 59–60
Life size mounts
skinning procedure,
240–242
Life span, 21–22
Lightweight rifles, 145
Lips
skinning procedure, 246
Litter size, 21
Load
selection, 131
Lodges, 222
Quebec
photo, 224
Longbows, 161
arrows, 164
Loose mouth, 113
Louisiana
black bear photos, 13
Louisiana black bear, 12–13
Lung shots, 141
and bowhunting,
155–156, 157
illustrated, 142, 143
Lyman Great Plains Rifle, 169

M
Magnum
market use, 179–180
Maine
black bear photos, 149,
198, 213
Blue Hill area, 16
outfitters and guides
associations, 266
state contact information,
254
voter passed regulations,
73–74
Maine hunting shoe
L.L. Bean, 120
Manitoba
black bear photos, 150,
165
outfitters and guides
associations, 268
province contact
information, 262
Massachusetts

state contact information,
254
voter passed regulations,
73–74
Mating, 21
Mating season, 21
McKenzie bear targets,
158–159
Meat
preparation
caution, 248
for table, 247–249
preparation for storage
and shipping,
242–244, 245
freezer life, 248
Meat with sweetener
for baiting, 86
Mechanical release, 166
Michigan
state contact information,
254–255
voter passed regulations,
73–74
Migration, 25
Minnesota, 15
state contact information,
255
Molasses
for baiting, 86–87
Montana
bear identification test,
67–68
grizzly bear, 67
outfitters and guides
associations, 267
state contact information,
255
Mount
life-like
photo, 236
Mouse calls, 130
Mouth
skinning procedure, 245
Movement, 42
distance, 24
food factor, 39
Muzzleloaders, 133, 169–186.
See also specific
types
helpful items, 183
ignition systems, 171–175
range limitations, 173,
175–176
rifle twists, 174
scopes, 174, 186
sling, 185

Muzzle velocity, 147
Muzzy three-blade 125-grain
broadhead, 165
Myths, 3–7

N
Nature's Own, 94
Neck shots, 141
Nevada
outfitters and guides
associations, 267
New Brunswick
black bear photos, 137,
206
outfitters and guides
associations, 268
province contact
information, 262
Newfoundland
black bear photos, 148,
181
outfitters and guides
associations, 268
province contact
information, 263
New Hampshire
state contact information,
255–256
New Jersey
hunting season
requirements, 72
licensing requirements,
72–73
state contact information,
256
New Mexico
hound requirements,
71–72
outfitters and guides
associations, 266
state contact information,
256
New York
outfitters and guides
associations, 267
state contact information,
256–257
Nipple pick, 183
Nipple wrench, 183
Nocking point, 166
North America Hunting Club,
215
North Carolina
ideal habitat, 19
state contact information,
257
Northwest territories

province contact
information, 263
Nose
skinning procedure, 245
Nova Scotia
province contact
information, 263–264

O
Off-colored black bears, 14–18
Off-game, 113
Omnivores, 11, 35
Ontario
province contact
information, 264
Open, 113
Open sights
photo, 139
Oregon
state contact information,
257
voter passed regulations,
73–74
Outfitter
American type plan, 217
camp cooks, 218
choosing, 214–222
confirming dates in
advance, 221
cost, 219
deposit, 219
and field dressing, 233
vs. guided only, 218
licenses and tag
requirements, 218,
219–220
mode of transportation,
220
propellant availability,
220
references, 217
skinning responsibility,
219
success rate, 216
understand total cost, 217
use guides also, 229
Outfitters
and guides associations,
265–269
Overdraw bows, 160

P
Pacers, 51–52
Pacific Northwest, 12
Paw. *See* Foot
Paws
skinning procedure, 245

Peep sight, 139
Pelts
field care, 236
photo
early spring, 202
fall, 208
late spring, 203
ready for salting or
freezing, 246
salted and air drying,
247
Pennsylvania, 16, 18
ideal habitat, 19
state contact information,
257–258
Pennsylvania flintlock long rifle
photo, 170
Percussion muzzleloaders, 171
photo, 172, 173
propellant needed,
180–181
Permanent camps. *See* Lodges
Pigs of the Woods, 10
Plex-type crosshairs, 138
Plott, 115–117
photo, 115
Population, 27, 29
by state or province, 29–30
Portable stands, 105
Possibles bag
photo, 183
Post, 138
Practice
with bow
from elevated stand,
158–159
breathing, 134–135
shooting, 134–135
positions, 134, 135
Predator calling, 122–123,
128–129
Pre-loaders, 183
Pressure tree dog, 113
Priming pan, 171
Princess Royal Island, 12
Propellant, 170
determining amount
needed, 179–180
types, 181–183
PSE Fire Flight
photo, 160
PSE Nova Extreme
adjusting draw weight,
160–161
Pulley operated compound
bow, 159
Pup trainer, 113

Pyrodex, 182–183
form, 182
manufacturer, 182
sizes, 182

Q
Quebec
black bear photos, 208
lodge photo, 224
outfitters and guides
associations,
268–269
province contact
information, 264
Queen Charlotte Islands, 12
Quick loaders, 183
Quivers, 166

R
Rabbit calls, 130
Range, 27
Range area, 33
Rear-end shots, 144
and bowhunting, 156–157
Recurve bows, 161
arrows, 164
Redbone coonhounds, 117
Redbone hound, 116
Remoteness
sex determination, 63
Reproduction rate, 26
Rifles, 131–152
calibers
list, 151–152
Rig dog, 112, 117–118
Rogers, Lynn, 10, 15
Roman legend of Callisto, 4–5
Roundballs
caliber comparison
photo, 176
caliber *vs.* distance, 176
proper powder charge,
179
range limitations, 175, 176
Rubs, 54
Rug mounts
skinning procedure,
240–242
Running silent, 114
Russell Pond Outfitters, 11

S
Saboted slugs, 187
Saddle bags, 117
Saskatchewan
outfitters and guides
associations, 269

Index

province contact
information,
264–265
Scat, 34, 42–47
amount, 43
color, 43–45
concentrations, 47
consistency, 45
dehydration rate, 46
freshness determination,
46
from grasses, 46
grizzly *vs.* black bear, 46
home range, 47
indicator of eating habits,
44
information learned from,
42–43
from meat, 45
photo, 43, 45
summer bedding, 47
time factor, 45
Scent drag, 114
Scent trails
commercial products, 93
creation, 85–86
Scientific classification, 10,
12–13
Scopes
magnification, 136–138
mount, 138
settings, 137–138
Scouting technique and tools,
20, 40–41
orchard owners, 41
rubs and tree markings,
54–55
scat, 42–47
time and effort involved,
42
tracks, 47–53
and trails, 56–57
for treestands, 100–101
See-through mounts
pros and cons, 138
Sex determination, 61–63
Sexual maturity, 21
Shooting distances
cartridges and bullet
weight, 151–152
Shooting down
and bowhunting, 157
Short-barrel weapons
photo, 190
Shot placement, 140–145
importance of, 132, 230
bowhunting, 155–156

Shoulder blades
and shot placement, 144
Sidelock muzzleloaders, 171
photo, 172
propellant needed,
180–181
scopes, 186
star type capper
photo, 185
Sight system, 136–140
bowhunting, 166–167
check out
on camp arrival, 227
muzzleloaders, 174
Silent, 114
Sire, 114
Size, 17
female or sow, 18
sex determination, 62
sows *vs.* boars, 19
Skinning, 239–242
basic cuts, 241
importance of quickness,
239
procedure
for various mounts,
240–242
and salting, 246
and temperature concern,
244
Skull
size, 140
Slick tree, 114
Slug guns, 186–187
range limitations, 187
Smelling, 23–24
Smith, Richard, 238
Solid lead conicals, 179
South Carolina
ideal habitat, 19
state contact information,
258
Sows
vs. boars
head, 58–59
hibernation period, 25
hibernation period
ending, 210
size, 19
with cubs
killing prohibited, 61
harvesting
Wyoming, 72
in heat, 62
identification, 61–63
size, 18
Speed loaders, 183

Spot and stalk techniques
day packing items, 226
least expensive, 213–214
physical endurance,
226–228
Spotting scopes, 123–124
Spring hunts
insect repellent, 103
Spring seasons, 200–206
bear size, 206
Canadian provinces
allowing, 199
insects, 205
meat quality, 205–206
pelt condition, 201–204
productiveness, 200–201
states allowing, 198
weather conditions,
204–205
Squaring procedure, 51
St. Hubert hounds, 116
St. Joe National Forest, 15
Stabilizing binoculars, 124
Stalking
and still hunting, 125
Stand placement. *See also*
Treestands
in reference to baiting, 83
Still hunting, 122, 125–127
tactics, 126
Stillness
importance of, 106–107
Stop and stalk
hunting method, 122–125
Straight-line capper, 185
photo, 185
Stride, 52
Strike, 114
Strike dog, 112, 117–118
String tracker, 230

T
Tab, 166
Teeth
number of, 22
photo, 22
Tennessee
state contact information,
258
Tent camps, 222
vs. lodges, 222–223
photo, 216, 223
Testicles
identification, 62
Thompson/Center Hawken
photo, 173, 180
Tight mouth, 114

T-Loader, 183–184
  photo, 184
Tolbot hounds, 116
Track drifter, 114
Tracking
  bears, 127, 128
  downed bears, 230–233
  importance of blood,
    233
Tracking in snow, 122, 127–128
Tracks, 47–53
  front
    and squared hide size
    determination, 49
  grizzly vs. black bear,
    52–53
  hind vs. front
    size, 48
  males vs. females, 49
  measuring, 47–48, 50
  photo, 48
  shape, 48
Track straddler, 114
TRAFFIC, 29
Trails, 56–57
Traveling, 42
  sex determination, 63
Treed bark, 114
Treed bear, 121–122
Treeing Walkers, 116
Trees, 53–56
  and bedding area, 58
  bite marks, 54
  deciduous and
    coniferous, 54
  fresh markings, 54
  home range, 54
  rubs, 54
  types for bears, 53
  used for, 55
Treestands, 100–108
  building
    timing, 101, 102
  comfort consideration, 101
  vs. ground blind, 101
  height and distance
    from baiting, 104–105
  hunter
    patients, 107
    stillness, 106–107

placement for
  bowhunting, 157
  wind current
    consideration, 101
Tremarctine bears, 12
Trichinella spiralis, 248
Trigger pull
  setting, 135–136
Triple Seven, 183
Trophy, 64–66
  color, 65–66
  definition, 64
  female, 65
  indications, 64
  measuring, 64
  record book minimums,
    64

U
Underfur, 20
  photo, 202
United States
  black bear hunting
    seasons, 199
  leaving
    gun registration
    requirements, 221
  population, 29–30
Ursus americanus
  species and subspecies,
    10, 12–13
  marking and color,
    14–15
  range area, 13
Ursus arctos horribilis, 66
Utah
  state contact information,
    258–259

V
Vancouver Island, 12
Variable scopes, 137–138
Velocity, 147
Vermont
  state contact information,
    259
Virginia
  ideal habitat, 19
  state contact information,
    259

Virginia hounds, 116
Vision, 23
Vocal repertoire, 22–23

W
Walkers, 116
  photo, 115
Walkie-talkies
  hound hunting,
    119–120
Walking stride, 52
Wallows, 56–57
Washington
  bag limits, 73
  outfitters and guides
    associations, 267
  state contact information,
    260
  voter passed regulations,
    73–74
Water grounds, 56–57
Weaning, 21
Weight gain, 33
West Virginia
  state contact information,
    260
Wide hunter, 114
Wildlife biologists
  restricting authority,
    74–75
  scouting tool, 41
Wildlife Buffet, 94
Wisconsin
  bait requirements, 71
  bear size, 17
  state contact information,
    260–261
Wyoming
  outfitters and guides
    associations, 266
  sow harvesting, 72
  state contact information,
    261

Y
Yukon
  outfitters and guides
    associations, 268
  province contact
    information, 265